MW00795938

RESULTS
DRIVEN
ORGANIZATIONS

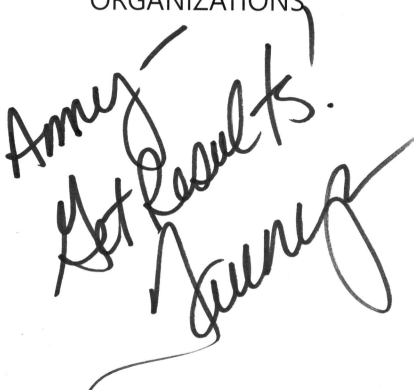

Amy -

Get Results.

Dr. Taunya Lowe is masterful...
- JOE THEISMANN
Legendary NFL World Champion Quarterback • NFL Football TV Commentator

RESULTS
DRIVEN
ORGANIZATIONS

THE 4 KEYS FOR A
HIGH PERFORMANCE WORKPLACE

Taunya A. Lowe, Ph.D.

Copyright @ 2019 Taunya A. Lowe, Ph.D.

All rights reserved.

No part of this book may be reproduced, distributed, or transmitted in any form by any means, graphic, electronic, or mechanical, including photocopy, recording, taping, or by any information storage or retrieval system, without permission in writing from the author, except in the case of reprints in the context of reviews, quotes, or references.

Printed in the United States of America

ISBN: 978-1-643-169-217

What Others are Saying About Dr. Taunya Lowe & Her Strategies

"If you're ready to positively transform your life, then read and absorb the strategies in this brilliant book by my friend Dr. Taunya Lowe! Dr. Lowe truly cares about helping others and her ideas will make a positive difference in your life!"

James Malinchak
Featured on ABCs Hit TV Show, "Secret Millionaire"
Authored 20 Books, Delivered 3,000 Presentations & 1,000 Consultations
Best-Selling Author, Millionaire Success Secrets
Founder, www.MillionaireFreeBook.com

Dr. Taunya Lowe is a master of explaining valuable skills that are highly necessary for business. This revolutionary book outlines a clear strategy for companies, and business professionals to implement seamlessly. Thoroughly enjoyed the read and will be implementing steps for my team. I highly recommend her for anyone that is managing a team.

Theresa Casey Hayes
MHRM, Human Resources Director
National Restaurant Chain

As a partner to your success, Dr. Taunya Lowe adds value, to your organization using her expertise while integrating real life experiences into her methodology.

Kevin Harrington
Original Shark on the Hit TV Show Shark Tank,
Pioneer of the As Seen on TV Industry

Dr. Taunya Lowe cuts to the chase and gently places the rubber on the road of outcome focused organizations. She reminds us that the target drives the activity and not the other way around. Ingest this dose of brilliance at your earliest convenience.

Rod Brown
Chief Operating Officer OnceLogix,
Forbes Best Small Company Inc. 5000 List

Dr. Taunya Lowe is masterful at helping employees self-identify their workplace behavior challenges and build a strategy for improved performance and success.

Joe Theismann
Legendary NFL World Champion Quarterback
NFL Football TV Commentator
Featured in the Hit Movie, The Blind Side

Taunya Lowe provides an easy read filled with personal experiences and proven techniques. This is a great foundational guide or "how-to" manual for anyone wanting to be a leader of people or any organization wanting to make a step-function improvement in performance. Dr. Taunya Lowe provides reflections/insights on teaming, why we run from it, and what it takes to be good at it.

Rodger Benson
Senior Operations Manager
Sandy Run Roasting Plant, Starbucks Coffee Company

Dr. Taunya Lowe's Results Driven Philosophy will transform your organization one department at a time.

Patty Aubery,
#1 NY Times Best Selling Author
Past President, Chicken Soup for the Soul
Co-Founder, The Jack Canfield Companies

Lessons learned from the wise prove exponential in their influence. Dr. Taunya Lowe has a profound way of helping people grow in many facets of business and in life.

Walter Brooks
Founder and Chief Executive Office
StarBQ House Franchising
3 Brothers BBQ

"This book is the secret weapon that every organization and leader can use to achieve success in business. Dr. Lowe has put together a collection of the four keys and organizational success strategies, in an easy to read guide. Her book is incredibly noteworthy and valuable to help you achieve a high-performance workplace and the results that every business and organization strives for to be successful. "Results Driven Organizations" is truly magical! Well done!"

John Formica (The Ex-Disney Guy)
One of the World's Foremost Disney Philosophy Experts
America's Best Customer Experience Speaker, Trainer, Coach

Dedication

This book is dedicated to all of the organizations who are committed to excellence. To the organizations who are invested in creating an organizational culture that will yield opportunities for success, significance and a high performing workplace.

Motivate and Inspire Others

Share This Book!

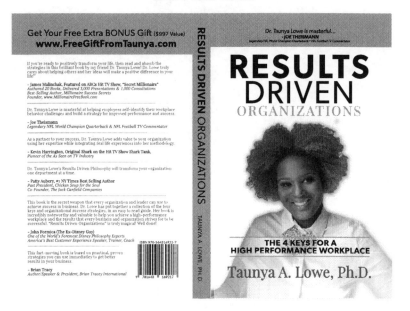

Retail $24.95

Bulk Order Discounts

5-20 books	$21.95
21-99 Books	$18.95
100-499 Books	$15.95
500-999 Books	$10.95
1,000+ Books	$8.95

To place an order contact

678-451-4259

support@drtaunyalowe.com

www.drtaunyalowe.com

THE IDEAL PROFESSIONAL SPEAKER FOR YOUR NEXT EVENT!

Organizations that want to develop their teams, leaders, and potential leaders hire Dr. Taunya Lowe for workshops, training, executive coaching and consulting

TO CONTACT OR BOOK DR. TAUNYA LOWE:

678-451-4259

support@drtaunyalowe.com

www.drtaunyalowe.com

Table of Contents

Foreword

You may remember me from being featured on the hit ABC TV show, "Secret Millionaire." If you do not know of the show, here is the basic premise from show promotions:

"What happens when business motivational speaker and self-made millionaire James Malinchak is picked up by an ABC television crew, placed on an airplane with no money, credit cards, cell phone, laptop or watch, and is whisked off to an impoverished neighborhood, where he had to survive on $44.66 cents for a week?

The show features Malinchak leaving his current lifestyle in search of real-life heroes who are making a difference in their local community. He ultimately reveals himself as a millionaire and rewards them with a portion of his own money to further their cause by gifting them with checks of his own money totaling over $100,000. If you watched ABC's 'Secret Millionaire' you know that James is no ordinary entrepreneur. He is a self-made millionaire with a strong passion for giving back and serving others."

Amazingly, over 10 MILLION people watched me on the show! Whether I am speaking at a conference, walking through an airport, consulting for an entrepreneur or just hanging out at a coffee shop, I always seem to get asked the same question. "What was it like being on Secret Millionaire when you had to live undercover in an impoverished neighborhood and how did it affect you?"

My answer is always the same.

The greatest gift you can have is when you simply give in order to help and serve others. There is no better feeling than when you know you have made a positive difference in lives of others.

And that is exactly what my friend Dr. Taunya Lowe and her teachings can do for you! She will inspire you through sharing her wisdom and personal experiences.

Dr. Lowe is an author, speaker and leader who truly cares about making a positive difference in the lives of others.

In this book you will be inspired by her genuine, caring nature for making a difference in your life. And her strategies can help you to achieve more than ever before.

Some strategies may comfort you while others may challenge your old paradigm. One thing is for certain. Dr. Lowe and her strategies will stamp your spirit with an abundance of love, hope and encouragement so you can reach new levels of courage, fulfillment and personal happiness.

It is my sincere honor to introduce to you Dr. Lowe and her amazing book!

James Malinchak
Featured on ABCs Hit TV Show, "Secret Millionaire"
Authored 20 Books, Delivered 3,000 Presentations & 1,000 Consultations
Best-Selling Author, Millionaire Success Secrets
Founder, www.MillionaireFreeBook.com

CONGRATULATIONS

Welcome to the 3%! Do you know that only 3% of people invest in themselves in order to grow to their next level? Well, you just joined the ranks of that special group of people who made an intentional decision to take their organization to the next level by focusing on a results-driven philosophy. Congratulations!

Who am I? I am a Consultant who loves taking organizations to their next level by helping them strengthen their workforce to excel in 4 primary areas of organizational success; strategy, leadership, team building, and customer experiences.

My passion for training, speaking, and developing all started when I was in college. I found myself in consultative and training roles as a student, an intern, and even a volunteer.

I went into organizations like a sponge often leaving with more questions than insights.

Questions like:

- Why aren't people happy with their jobs?

- Why doesn't their mission reflect the organization?

- Why are people leaving at alarming rates?

- Why is this organization so unorganized?

- Is it ok to sleep at your desk and read the newspaper for most of the day (seriously this actually happened)?

- If the budgets are being cut, why all this wasteful spending?

And so many more questions.

I knew early that I wanted to be a consultant even when I wasn't sure exactly what a consultant was or what they did, but I met one at a College Career Day, and I knew that I wanted to do what this person did. I later got an internship in that same organization and was totally disappointed in what I saw on the inside, but I learned much more than I ever expected.

I was a sponge, and I soaked up everything; every meeting, every technique, how people were treated. I was always listening, watching, learning, and experiencing.

Sometimes the experiences provided phenomenal lessons, and sometimes they provided horrible nightmares, but lessons nonetheless. I was stretching, I was growing.

After college, the journey began, and yes it has indeed been a journey. A data-collecting journey if you will. Who knew I would go on to work for a variety of organizations? I worked for small government-funded organizations, large nonprofit organizations, county government, state government, academia, corporate, and as a Consultant in my own firm.

One may think, wow she has a lot of jobs, but they were not just jobs, they were training camps - learning opportunities. I have had opportunities to learn about operations, budgets, communication, strategy, leadership, teamwork, and customer experiences. I have also had opportunities to develop and craft my results-driven philosophy for high-performance workplaces. I have had opportunities to learn from the bes, do research and compile a wealth of knowledge for more than 20 years.

For more than 20+ years, I've had the opportunity to work for, consult with, and counsel a variety of organizations that struggled with meeting outcomes and maintaining an environment of excellence, because they didn't have a clear strategy, leadership needed support and development, teams were not committed, and their internal and external customer experiences were challenged.

When I enter an organization, I'm not teaching new information. The thing about information is that it is plentiful and abundant, thanks to the web. So although the information may not be new information, many organizations are challenged with the application of information.

I nurture CEOs, Managers, Team Leads, Pastors, and Executive Directors and help them apply information in the best manner for their organization to obtain the best results. Information is plentiful; application is not.

If you're reading this book, it means that you are serious about creating a culture of excellence, a culture of high performers, and a culture of consistency, intentional change and growth for your organization.

It's only when all four keys exist in tandem that workplaces will yield high performance.

I'm often asked the question, "Is everyone capable of operating at a high level?" My answer is YES! If you maximize the strengths you have and allocate your resources accordingly, you can perform at a high level based on where you are. Everyone in your organization should be functioning at the maximum level of their capacity while you are steadily growing to your next level.

When you have an organization of people who are capable but are only operating on 30-40% of their ability, it most definitely affects the workforce, the teams, the productivity, the goals, the outcomes, the service, and the profits.

My hope is that this resource will strengthen you and your teams desire for high performance.

Results-Driven Strategic Planning

"The best CEOs I know are teachers, and at the core of what they teach is strategy."
— Michael Porter

Results-Driven Strategic Planning

As I work with my clients in both the coach and consultant role, I've discovered there is a real need for creating and developing results-driven strategies. It's one thing to have a vision, it's another to develop a step-by-step plan as to how you will get it done and who will be involved. The design of the plays, the input of the coordinates into the GPS, and the unfolding of the roadmap that will put you in the direction of manifesting your organizational mission and vision into reality.

I liken the change strategy to baking bread. There are several components needed to bake bread, and sometimes, many times, you are going to get dirty with all of the flour, but in the end, you will have a delicious loaf of bread, if you follow all of the steps. Sometimes it takes several tries to get the bread just like you want it, but you can't give up; adjust the recipe and bake again; try different flour, and bake again.

Results-Driven Strategy requires 3 things:

The first is a commitment to the "get dirty" factor, meaning not being afraid to get down and dirty in the "flour" to develop a roadmap for your organization. This is where the work begins.

The second is determining your thinking style and moving toward becoming a strategic thinker. Results-Driven Strategic planning requires that you think differently, innovatively, creatively, and limitlessly. Michael Stanleigh, CEO of Business Improvement Architects, defines strategic thinking as "a planning process that applies innovation, strategic planning, and operational planning to develop strategies that have a greater chance for success. Strategic thinking is the "what" and "why" of the planning process. It answers the question, "What should I be doing, and why?" Strategic Thinking requires innovation and creativity and includes a research phase."

How can you tell if you are a strategic thinker? Compare these eight characteristics and their opposite to determine your strategic thinking style, as well as the strategic thinking style of your organization and your organizational leaders.

STRATEGIC THINKERS	NON-STRATEGIC THINKERS
Future -based: Anticipate change and look for opportunities that may arise, or looking through the turn	**Reactive:** Often wait to be told what to do or what action to take, and rarely initiate ideas.
Curious: Interested in what is going on throughout their department, company, industry and the larger business environment.	**Isolated:** Typically work without input from others or without understanding others' goals and objectives.
Good steward of resources: Willing to put in extra time today in order to gain a better outcome tomorrow.	**Focusing on cost:** Sometimes unwilling to make a good investment and do not consider the potential overall impact or long-term goals.
Risk Taker: Are not limited to the past or current thinking and are willing to try new methods. They brainstorm ideas and prefer to try something new.	**Cautious:** Normally are only interested in maintaining the status quo.
Urgent and important: Do not equate busy with effective and place a higher value on projects with potential for a greater impact and return.	**Unable to prioritize:** Often treat all tasks equally without regard to impact.
Nimble: Able to adjust and modify their approach based on circumstances.	**Inflexible:** May be unwilling to alter their plans even when adjustments could yield a better return.
Life-long learner: Willing to be taught, proactively seeking knowledge and skills, and willing to teach others.	**Satisfied:** Normally not interested in learning new things or methods and are content with their current capabilities.
Creative: Consider outrageous ideas and will think outside the box.	**Predictable:** Often stick with paths that are familiar

Adapted from Woolsey, Blake. "8 Characteristics of a Strategic Thinker." Bright Thoughts 12 July 2012 http://blog.mitchcommgroup.com/blake/8-characteristics-of-a-strategic-thinker/.

Creating an organization of strategic thinkers requires a culture shift. Increasing opportunities for curiosity, taking risks, being creative and operating in a system that provides constant learning opportunists. As you review this list, think about who the people are in your organization at all levels. Those are the people who should participate in results-driven strategic planning.

Finally, the plan, putting the what and why into the how and the who. How are the action steps that you will take to reach the goal in order to manifest the vision, and who will you solicit to help you for support, accountability, resources, and motivation? When this is complete, you will be one step closer to achieving organizational success.

Every organization wants massive results, and they want them yesterday, but many organizations want them without putting in the groundwork and spending the time necessary to obtain massive, epic, earth-shattering results.

Here are a few examples:

Client #1: A mega-church had been in existence for more than 15 years. They were doing major projects in the community and in the church, but they were not getting the results they really desired. They were not reaching the populations they really wanted to reach. Why? In more than 15 years, they never participated in strategic planning, because they were event-based instead of strategy-based.

Client #2: A Nonprofit Organization with an operational budget of $10,000,000.00, a residential facility for males struggling with addiction. They were working on a 3-year accreditation, but they had not really used any of the growth methods and indicators from 3 years prior. Why? Their strategic plan was basically a checkbox and file item on their to do list. Staff had turned over many times and, no one ever thought about making the strategic plan apart from on-boarding. Hence, another epic fail when it came to obtaining massive, epic, earth-shattering results on an ongoing basis.

Finally, **Client #3:** A major player in the insurance industry had a huge undertaking with hiring and training staff to receive customer calls accurately as the Affordable Health Care Act was being rolled out across the country. There was no strategy. There were a lot of issues. Productivity was minimal, and key staff people lost their jobs. Why? There were progress gaps due to poor planning and execution (process and progress gaps). They are experiencing these gaps because they had not taken the time to lay the foundation (preparation) for their major project and, in turn, used a Band-Aid approach in order to avoid correcting problems at the root. Several things kept them further and further away from experiencing small milestones of success as they forged toward the big outcome. It was a constant struggle to keep the train on the track in order to avoid the train wreck that was quickly approaching.

As you can see from the three examples, I've worked with a variety of organizations, and I've found that it doesn't matter the type of organization, everything begins and ends with planning. Not just any planning, but results-driven strategic planning.

WHAT IS RESULTS-DRIVEN STRATEGIC PLANNING?

Strategic planning is a method of planning a series of events in an organized manner in order to accomplish an organizations team's, or department's goal. In order for this type of planning to prove meaningful, you must look at the entire picture of your organization (not just the good parts) and then design SMART steps to maneuver getting to the finish line. For example, we could say that the strategy is to overtake an area while the tactical planning is how you will fight each battle. The strategy is the plan to get to the desired outcome.

Now, let's look at this in terms of results-driven strategic planning. Strategic planning can work in many ways in any organization. For example, you may want to create a plan to get your department, team, or the entire organization from one level to the next. Depending on what that is, you can create a plan for key players to follow to achieve the end results.

Here are a few examples of what strategic planning would look like in different departments of an organization:

- Financial aspects, such as profit, loss, increasing sales, or lowering costs.

- In human resources, you can devise a strategic plan to recruit new hires, to promote individuals, to staff a location quickly and for retention.

- You can use strategic planning for your marketing plans. How you will market, where you will market, and how much you will spend in those areas are all determined through the strategic planning.

What is strategy?

Let's break this down even more. As soon as I learned to play golf, I fell in love with it because it is a game of strategy. I can relate how I move on the golf course to things that happen in organizations. Not keeping my head down when I am about to drive from the tee box almost always causes my ball to go in the opposite direction that I want it to go. Same thing happens in organizations if we don't keep our eye on the mission, vision, key players, and the overall outcome. You will not achieve your desired outcomes. For me, that means my ball ends up in the trees, in someone's yard, or just a few inches away from me. However, in an organization, this could mean loss of productivity, loss of staff, and ultimately loss of profits.

So what is strategy?

Strategic planning is not strategy. Strategy is the "what" you and your organization are going to be, and the broad approach to how you are going to do that. Strategic Planning looks at the details of how you will get there, which associations you will joint-venture with, how many salespeople you will add this year, what type of advertising you will use, whether to pay for page-views or click-throughs.

The strategic plan will itemize the specific actions you will take in a given time frame, and the specific results those actions will produce. Strategy defines the destination, and whether you will take a scenic way or a fast way, and if you want rest stops. Strategic planning identifies the specific highways and the specific streets.

Have you bothered to think about where you want to go recently? Most organizations and entrepreneurs started with an idea of what they wanted to create or what problem they were going to solve. That may have been a long time ago. Perhaps it's time for you to consider those questions again.

STRATEGY IS NOT A SET OF PREFERENCES

Many companies think strategy is about evaluating preferences or a set of options. These preferences or options are often discussed in terms of available resources, or a competitive response. Organizations say things like - "We have only 12 development resources available to us, which means we can bring two key program feature sets to market, and XYZ Co. has just announced compatibility with our databases. What are we going to do?" These discussions and thought processes are limiting, and many times, cause the planning process to get stuck and the creative process to stop which result in falling back into old behaviors.

STRATEGY IS NOT INCREMENTAL

Organizations also consider strategy in terms of increments. Last year, you increased profits by 20%; does that mean this year you should shoot for increasing profits by 20%? Or 25%? Or, since you added three new modules last year, and reduced customer response time by 33%, should you plan to do the same, or something a bit better, this year?

It's been said that insanity is doing the same thing over and over again, expecting different results. When you do the same things, only better, only harder, only more, only smarter, what you'll get is more of what you've already got. That's fine, as long as you've determined that more of what you've got is appropriate for this stage of your organization's life cycle.

Strategy is an invention

Strategy is designing your path, your play, your next move. Your strategy is a statement of what you will do as an organization to realize your organizational vision: what specifically will you accomplish, what meaning will your organization have, and how will you create relationships, value, and profits.

Don't ignore your past results.

Don't allow your strategy to be constrained by them.

Don't ignore the marketplace.

Don't fall into the trap of letting your competitors' actions define what yours will be.

Certainly, don't ignore your customers – Don't think that your customers' wants and desires are the only measures of what you should seek to accomplish.

These references; past results, markets, competitors, customers, must be taken into account. What it boils down to is this: your strategy is the direction your organization will take, because you said so.

An invented strategy inspires you because it fulfills your vision for your company, and because you see how the realization of your strategy makes an important difference in the world, it inspires your team, your customers, and your prospects.

An invented strategy energizes all your constituents, where incrementalism just seems like more work. An invented strategy can propel your enterprise to greatness.

An invented strategy can call forth achievements beyond what you currently consider possible. Breakthroughs and blockbusters are never founded on incremental improvement.

Invented strategies can change your organization's relationship to the marketplace and to the world.

Inventing Results-Driven Strategy

The route to inventing strategy is simple – it involves asking the right questions.

- What direction can the organization take now to realize your vision?

- What value proposition will you offer customers?

- What meaningful difference will you make in your marketplace?

- What meaningful difference will you make in your world?

- How do you want to affect the lives of your people, your customers, your clients, your family?

Are you building something totally new, or are you improving an existing idea? What are the dimensions of the impact you want to have? Will it be faster? Better? Cheaper? Easier? Safer? More luxurious? More convenient? More portable? More entertaining? More universal?

Next, from a high-level perspective, how will you mobilize your resources and time your maneuvers to offer that value and make that difference.

When you answer these questions, then you are on the road to inventing your Results-Driven Strategy.

There are no rules in strategy

We are a society filled with rules. We tend to maintain archaic organizational rules and refuse to break the rules that will yield results. Strategy is like that. Strategy is not evolutionary; it is revolutionary. Don't assume the old rules apply or let them guide your thinking. Breaking rules may actually be a way to conceive of strategy. Ask yourself, "What rules can we break?" Consider which obsolete beliefs restrain growth in your company or in your market. Make up your own assumptions. Breaking the rules, certainly doesn't advocate that you break the law, but ignoring some societal norms and going ahead with what your gut instinct and knowledge indicates is right, is acceptable and preferable. Being a conformist holds you back from experiencing massive, epic, earth-shattering results and what would ultimately be the best move for your organization. The Dalai Lama XIV teaches, "Know the rules well, so you can break them effectively."

Don't rush implementation

Many organizations get stuck in the strategy process and truly consider every viable opportunity because they begin to switch gears to implementation while in the middle of strategy. While you are considering strategy, don't worry about what you have and don't have in order to implement what you are thinking about. If you switch gears too soon, you will begin to sabotage your direction and the planning process from the beginning. This is challenging for many people in the strategy process. There will be plenty of room for compromise later, if you must. Ignore the resource constraints that haunt you throughout the year and dare to dream. Reality will come soon enough. Author Gary Hamil suggests that one definition of strategy include the "...quest to overcome resource constraints through a creative and unending pursuit of better resource leverage."

IMPLEMENTATION

You've finally arrived at implementation. Once you have formulated a strategy you believe will make a difference and lead to greater returns, you have to figure out how to make it happen given all the constraints you operate under. That is where the strategic and tactical planning comes in. The strategic planning should take place in phases, several operating concurrently depending on who is involved.

When I work with organizations, I collect data in phases. I conduct discovery sessions to find out exactly what you want, where you want to go, what's been done before, who was involved, who will be involved this time, and develop timelines. Anything you and I can possibly think of to get as much information before the process begins. I also conduct assessments. Some assessments can take place while other things are being done. Assessments provide a picture of the strength in the organization. Many organizations don't understand the strength of their people because they don't know or they don't ask. They don't understand how they have grown or if they have become stagnant and bored.

I use the Wiley 363 and DiSC assessment to collect data on who is in the organization, how they work, how they work with others, and where their growth areas are. All key elements during the planning phase. I will go into more detail about the DiSC assessment in the Results-Driven Team section.

While data is coming in from the 363 and the DiSC, I am completing SWOT and Gap analysis with key players and leadership to gather data for constructing the results driven strategy.

Once you collect the results, the remaining components of the strategy are developed for the action plan. The components of a strategic plan consists of the following but are not limited to:

*GAP ANALYSIS

In management literature, *gap analysis* involves the comparison of actual performance with potential or desired performance. If an organization does not make the best use of current resources, or forgoes investment in capital or technology, it may produce or perform below its potential. *Strategic gap analysis* is an evaluation of the difference between the desired outcome and actual outcome, and what must be done to achieve the desired goal. After conducting this analysis, the company should develop an implementation plan (also known as an operational plan) to eliminate the gaps.

*SWOT ANALYSIS

The reason to include a SWOT analysis (analysis of your Strengths, Weaknesses, Opportunities, and Threats) in your Strategic Plan is to help you determine the best opportunities to pursue to achieve your growth goals. It also helps you identify which strengths you must develop in the near future to improve your company.

* MISSION

Defining the mission is key because it is the mission that should drive the organization. Internal and external customers should feel the mission when engaging with everyone within the organization. The mission encourages an organization to develop a brief description of the purpose to inform potential stockholders, employees, and customers what they can expect from the company. From the mission definition, a mission statement can be developed that serves as a company's calling card and core focus description.

* Vision/Trend Analysis

The next facet of Results-Driven Strategic Planning directs a company to analyze current market trends and make committed decisions about where the business is heading. Defining long-term goals and visualizing the future of the organization can help to focus current activities and important financial decisions.

* Strategic Objectives

Once long-term goals have been set, the strategic objectives phase consists of formulating actual business plans to achieve the visualized goals. One acronym frequently used in this stage of Strategic Planning Steps is SMART.

SMART stands for the type of objectives to be developed to fully realize the company's long-term goals. These objectives include:

- S – Specific objectives

- M – Measurable objectives

- A – Achievable objectives

- R – Resource-based, realistic objectives

- T – Time-frame assessed objectives

* Critical Success Factors: Important milestones and achievements are key to goal realization and should be identified as the critical success factor stage of Results-Driven Strategic Planning. Singling out these factors provides an easy means for measuring the ongoing success of the business plan.

* Actions to be implemented: After critical success factors have been identified, the next phase involves the development of action plans needed to realize success. Specific tasks and organization

management strategies are designed to effectively implement the business plan. Task management is often defined by the core competencies required for each position in the company.

* Performance Analysis and Progress Measurement: The last of the most common steps is comprised of formulating methods by which to measure the organization's progress. Comprehensive performance analysis tools and measurement criteria are developed to effectively monitor the success of the current system. These tools can be used to report both internally and externally on the progress and growth of the company.

"We need to make some big changes around here.
The kind of changes where many decisions are
made but nothing actually happens."

Results-Driven Leadership

"Leadership is the lifting of a man's vision to higher sights, the raising of a man's performance to a higher standard, the building of a man's personality beyond its limitations.

—Peter Drucker"

Results-Driven Leadership

eadership. What is leadership? I googled the word leadership and I found 2,120,000,000 results that led me to articles and definitions from Forbes, Inc., TedTalks, Psychology Today and so many more. However, when you close the curtain, and you really take a moment to ponder it, the question continues to linger. What IS leadership, really?

For many, it is a huge word with a lot of responsibility that people run from as often as possible. For others, it's the missing Cinderella slipper; it's a perfect fit, which flows naturally and with ease. Then, there are those who spend time developing and training to become a 'good' leader, an effective leader reading book after book and attending training after training and completing certification after certification as though they were preparing for a triathlon.

You don't have to lead an army or a country to benefit from results-driven leadership skills. Learning these skills can help you become a better person and a leader in your organization and your area of expertise. Think about the leaders you admire (in history or your own life), what is it about them that makes them standout to you? What leadership knowledge can you gain from them to help you lead others?

So what is leadership? In Lolly Daskal's 2016 Inc. Magazine article, Daskal documented 100 answers to the question, what is leadership?

HERE ARE 10 OF MY FAVORITE:

- The ultimate measure of a man is not where he stands in moments of comfort, but where he stands at times of challenge and controversy." - *Martin Luther King Jr*

- "It is better to lead from behind and to put others in front, especially when you celebrate victory when nice things occur. You take the front line when there is a danger. Then people will appreciate your leadership." - *Nelson Mandela*

- "Leadership defines what the future should look like, aligns people with that vision, and inspires them to make it happen, despite the obstacles." - *John Kotter*

- "Leadership is an opportunity to serve. It is not a trumpet call to self-importance." - *J. Donald Walters*

- "Management is about arranging and telling. Leadership is about nurturing and enhancing." - *Tom Peters*

- "Leadership is a potent combination of strategy and character. But if you must be without one, be without the strategy." - *Norman Schwarzkopf*

- "Leadership is unlocking people's potential to become better." - *Bill Bradley*

- "The leadership instinct you are born with is the backbone. You develop the funny bone and the wishbone that go with it." - *Elaine Agather*

- "Leadership consists of picking good men [and women] and helping them do their best." - *Chester W. Nimitz*

- "While a good leader sustains momentum, a great leader increases it." – *John C. Maxwell*

My consensus is - leadership involves people; it's not a solo job, and it's not an opportunity to gain another single success. It's about mentoring, coaching, and developing others to greatness. I have met many people rushing to the "big chair" of leadership because of the position, the perceived status, the title, or even the financial increase, but none of that matters when you are leading your team, department, or entire organization on a quest. So let's start with what results-driven leadership is NOT.

RESULTS-DRIVEN LEADERSHIP IS NOT:

- Being a Boss

- Title

- Position

- Power

- Prestige

Results-Driven Leadership is AI. No, it is not artificial intelligence; it is action and influence. Leadership is about you and it is also not about you (I'll explain that in a moment). Leadership is about you as an individual, your values, your organizational commitment, and your philosophy. Leadership is also about what you plan to do for others, the organization and the people in the organization. What wins will you help them achieve? How will you lift the morale of the organization? How will you use your influence to develop more leaders?

RESULTS-DRIVEN LEADERSHIP IS:

- Personal Leadership Philosophy

- Creating Culture

- Developing More Leaders

- Legacy

PERSONAL LEADERSHIP PHILOSOPHY

It's not enough to know your leadership style. Leadership styles are limiting. Results-Driven Leaders understand that they must take an eclectic approach when it comes to leadership style as well as define their Personal Leadership Philosophy (PLP) and communicate it by living it passionately on a daily basis in words and actions. Results-Driven Leaders take the time to determine who they are, their values, and priorities. When you know your leadership philosophy, you also know your course of action and can lead others effectively. John Collins calls it "Level 5" leadership. Level 5 leadership is a concept developed in his book Good to Great. Level 5 leaders display a powerful mixture of personal humility and indomitable will. They're incredibly ambitious, but their ambition is first and foremost for the cause, for the organization and its purpose, not themselves. While Level 5 leaders can come in many personality packages, they are often self-effacing, quiet, reserved, and even shy. Collins shared, "Every good-to-great transition in our research began with a Level 5 leader who motivated the enterprise more with inspired standards than inspiring personality."

CREATING CULTURE

Creating culture is the most important job of a leader, not vision, not strategy, but culture because it is the most powerful factor in any organization. A leader should spend time creating a strong culture and making sure that it is consistent throughout the organization. Creating culture defines, "this is how we do things, here!" Which may mean for many organizations taking a look at just how we do things here, and adjust accordingly. Organizational culture may be toxic, or it may be a great culture to thrive; either way, it is the leader's job to establish a consistent culture and make sure that it is adopted by current, new, and future members of the workforce at every level.

In 2005, Richard Clark was thrust into the position of CEO for the pharmaceutical firm, Merck & Co immediately following the Vioxx recall and more than 27,000 people saying their family member or loved one had suffered injury or death from the drug. It was a dark time for the pharmaceutical giant's 114-year history. Nevertheless, even in the quagmire, Clark saw an opportunity and had a plan to turn the pharmaceutical giant around, and it started with the culture. "Merck and other companies were known for their scientific innovation, but were crippled by a culture that buried good ideas under layers of bureaucracy." "A crisis is a terrible thing to waste," said the CEO. Clark also stated in an Executive Leadership magazine article, "The fact is, culture eats strategy for lunch. You can have a good strategy in place, but if you don't have the culture and the enabling systems, the [negative] culture of the organization will defeat the strategy."

In Sam Chand's book, *The Leader's Guide to Organizational Management: Change Your Culture Change Everything,* Chand also quotes Clark by stating that a toxic culture will eat your vision and mission for lunch. It does not allow the mission or the vision to survive and thrive and positively replicate itself.

Chand describes seven key important factors that shape organizational culture. These seven keys are designed to help leaders explore culture, assess the current culture of their organization, as well as use the steps as a tool for change. Chand's 7 steps are:

1. CONTROL

Who is really in control of your project, the organization and the information? Delegating responsibility and accountability in an organization are not dirty words and are essential in organizations. However, it is important to understand that the person at the head of the table may not be the "power broker." This reminds me of when I worked for the county health department and would go into communities with the "community leader's name." I was always so infuriated, because I quickly learned that the people with the real or perceived decision making power were never the names on the list. In Chand's description of control, he states the first sign of a problem is when there are turf wars around information and processes. Although someone should have responsibility and hold people accountable, planning should be a group effort, and team members should be partners in the effort. This is where cross training is critical.

2. UNDERSTANDING

Understanding is the why behind the what. Everyone on a team should have a clear picture and understanding of the vision, how they contribute, the gifts and contributions of the team members and the way the team functions. Understanding is about communication.

3. LEADERSHIP

Organizations should be pipelines for growing and developing more leaders. Voila!

4. TRUST

Everything good and bad in an organization thrives on trust. Trust is the glue that makes everything good possible. Trust may be given freely once it's earned. Trust is fluid and takes time to build, but it can be destroyed in an instant. Trust can be shattered in an instant by a dramatic event. Poor integrity deteriorates trust and the organization culture.

5. Unafraid

"Organizations with healthy teams foster the perspective that failure isn't a tragedy and conflict isn't the end of the world. Great leaders welcome different opinions, as long as they are offered in good will and with an eye toward a solution." Translation, sequester the organizational bullies.

6. Responsive

Chand describes responsiveness as a consistent process for collaboration with open lines of communications. "Responsive teams don't focus on big goals and sweeping strategies. They develop the habit of taking care of the little things, like, returning calls promptly, responding to emails, and communicating decisions to everyone who needs to know when he or she needs to know."

7. Execution

Execution is working from top to bottom to meet the objective. It is each person being crystal clear about their role and how they connect to the project. When it comes to execution, there is no room for guesswork.

We have all been there at one point or another in our careers when time is spent on a goal or a deliverable and things don't happen as expected. The leadership team spends long hours agreeing on a 3 or 5 year strategy to improve the performance of the organization. Management teams work equally hard to come up with supportive annual budgets. Both teams populate long PowerPoint presentations and well-built exhaustive spreadsheet files, yet not much happens in terms of actual deliverables! Ambitious year-end targets are missed. Improvement curves continue to shift to the right. The process for the restructuring of the organization begins now.

Questions immediately arise as to why these events occur so often and include:

- What has gone wrong and why?

- Are the goals too aggressive?

- Are the visions and/or strategies inadequate?

- Are middle managers unable to execute?

- If the answer is yes to all these questions, then why is it so?

All are good questions, however, based on my experience, a key element that must be addressed when it comes to execution is the importance of strategic alignment.

Strategic alignment, put simply, is "everyone rowing in the same direction." The tighter the linkage and the better the alignment, the likelihood of flawless organization execution becomes stronger.

Strategic alignment has several advantages once implemented properly and practiced. Benefits include:

1. Allowing an efficient use of usually scarce resources.

2. Resulting in increased speed of execution, as a corollary.

3. Promoting team efforts towards common goals.

4. Escalating employees' motivation, giving them a keener sense of contribution to the results of their individual groups and of the corporation as a whole.

When I think about the culture of an organization, Chick-Fil-A immediately comes to mind because it doesn't matter the location, the city, or the town, you will receive the same friendly "I want to serve you" service. That service goes beyond customer service training, that service is ingrained in the culture of the organization.

It's a part of their purpose statement unapologetically as well as their core values.

Dee Ann Turner, VP of Corporate Talent for Chick-Fil-A, discussed her book, *It's My Pleasure*, in an interview about how talent and culture have driven the organization's success. She stated after the death of her father and Truett Cathy, founder of Chick Fil-A, she felt a void of the two most influential business mentors in her life.

She stated, "For 30 years, Truett had ingrained in me the people principles I discuss in *It's My Pleasure*, particularly the idea that the success of an organization is determined by its talent. I wanted to be sure that those of us who learned these principles that are core to Chick-fil-A's foundation and success did not forget what he taught. I also wanted to be sure that franchisees and employees that never knew Truett would know these core principles that he so highly valued."

When asked, what are the most important principles that differentiate the culture at Chick-fil-A? Turner responded, "Every organization has their own cultural principles that make them unique and sometimes, from organization to organization, the principles sound similar. The real key is how the behaviors of the people of the organization support the culture. The consistency with which the corporate purpose, mission, core values and guiding principles have been lived out at Chick-fil-A over generations is the key differentiator. Many organizations have a powerful purpose and meaningful missions. They have well-crafted core values and guiding principles. It is the ability to select, steward, and sustain talent that is willing and capable to consistently live out the collective cultural foundation that differentiates an organization."

Developing More Leaders

As Sam Chand stated, "Organizations should be pipelines for growing and developing more leaders." John Maxwell describes four reasons why leaders need to reproduce leaders:

- The organization's growth potential is directly related to its personnel potential.

- Those closest to the leader will determine the success of the leader.

- Every organization has a shortage of leaders.

- Leaders attract other leaders.

There are two important questions leaders need to ask themselves:

1. Am I developing my potential as a leader? This is an important question as a leader because if you are not operating from your growth plan, you cannot grow other leaders in the organization.

2. Am I helping other leaders develop their potential?

Legacy (Succession)

Leadership is truly about influence, relationships, and examples. What type of influence do you have in your organizations? How do you develop and nurture relationships? Are you leading by example? Casting vision and delegating is the easy part of leadership. It's the impression you leave on an organization that matters. See the Results-Driven Leadership Checklist in the appendix.

"To be honest, I know nothing about leading.
But it's okay because my team knows
nothing about following."

Results-Driven Team Building

Not Finance. Not Strategy. Not Technology. It is teamwork that remains the ultimate competitive advantage because it is so powerful and so rare.

-- Patrick Lencioni

Results-Driven Team Building

The key to reaching organizational success is to surround yourself with people who will co-create with you in order to reach the highest pinnacle points in your organization (your legacy points)! To exceed your present reach, you must surround yourself with people who will challenge you and hold you accountable to move beyond your comfort zone and stretch farther.

That's your team!

Your organizational vision and mission are too big for you to carry alone. There are people in your organization that have the skills, knowledge, and ability to take the organization to the next level and reach pinnacles. The people you need are already in your organization, but you are probably overlooking them because of your preconceived team experiences.

Hesitation regarding working with others may come from negative team dynamics. A study by the University of Phoenix found that nearly 70 percent of employees admitted to being part of a dysfunctional unit. The study also revealed that while 95 percent of those who have ever worked on a team believe teamwork serves a critical function in the workplace, however, more than three-quarters of employees would rather work alone.

WHY DO WE CHOOSE TO WORK ALONE OVER TEAMS?

Many people have horrible experiences working with teams, and it usually dates to the dreaded group project assignment in school. This group assignment has been given out for many, many years to middle school, high school, college, and some graduate students resulting in one epic fail. Forget the grade, once it's over, NO ONE EVER wants to participate in a group project of any kind EVER AGAIN!!

As children, we are taught to play together, share, and say nice things when we would rather not. I'm sure the goal was for us to learn to work together, but again there was another epic fail that we were not taught how to operate on a team, just play nice (hence the beginning of being politically correct).

Fast forward to our careers, now we must work with a team and lead teams, but the voice inside wants to run and hide. Subconsciously, we begin to feel the trauma from our last bad team experience, and we say, "I'd rather go it alone." Regardless of all the research on the effectiveness of teams, the memory of the last time haunts you, and you take those thoughts and feelings with you into your next team assignment. You and every team member sitting around the table dreading the idea or being placed on a team and wishing they could just work alone.

In John Maxwell's 17 Indispensable Laws of Teamwork, Maxwell describes 4 reasons we choose to work alone.

1) Ego-

For many years, I worked alone, and had some amazing solo successes. I grew to like being a team of one and all that came with it. Like what? The free fuel for my ego. I knew I was not just good but great at what I did; I was often the youngest, the most educated, and only woman of color. Maxwell says, "It marks a big step in your development when you come to realize that other people can help you do a better job than you could do alone."

2) Insecurity –

I never thought I was threatened by others; I enjoyed the banter of those equally as bright as me. What I didn't want was to share the spotlight or any of my solo success. I wore my success as a badge of honor. It was a win for the organization, but it was also a win I didn't have to share. Although I would help others gain as many wins as possible in their lane as long as they stayed out of mine. I clearly had a case of this is my ball, and I don't want to share it with you. Maxwell says, "some individuals fail to promote teamwork because they feel threatened by other people."

3) Naiveté –

Maxwell says, "Some people naively underestimate the difficulty of achieving big things." I knew that I needed other people in a "they can help me" kind of way, but never thought about them helping me master mountains because in my mind, I'd taken myself to great heights already. Who needed them?

4) Temperament –

Working alone for so many years, I truly didn't know how to share my "toys" with others. I wanted to win, and as I inherited team members, they became bi-products of the win instead of partners in the win. My focus was on being successful and showing that it could be done by ME. After all, those were the only examples I had in internships and early career opportunities. I really thought that was how it was done. There is a quote that says, people do what they see, and that couldn't be more the truth. As it relates to temperament, Maxwell describes this as some people are not very outgoing and simply do not think in terms of team building and team participation.

THE PROS AND CONS OF TEAMS SURVEY, 2017

I have my own experiences and assumptions about teams. Why they work and why they don't, and why people feel the way they do about working in teams. November 2017, I conducted an informal study to collect data to confirm my assumptions. I asked my social media networks on Facebook, LinkedIn, and Twitter to provide feedback.

The responses vigorously poured in, and I was overwhelmed by the feedback from this informal qualitative survey. The responses told me that people had opinions about this subject and wanted to share. My assumptions were confirmed, and I realized team development is and always will be a topic that needs not just training and passing along information, but it's a topic regardless of whether development takes place OR NOT; it will have a long-term effect on the culture of an organization.

When we leave teams in the hands of people instead of weaving it into the fabric, the core values of your organizations will never have consistency and productivity, and profits will always suffer.

So, let's look at a summary of the data responses. You can see all of the data responses in the appendix section.

The Pros and Cons of Teams Survey, 2017

Q1. WHAT HAS BEEN YOUR WORST EXPERIENCE WITH A TEAM?

- **Leadership**
  - o   Poor Leader
  - o   Leader didn't listen

- o Leader was not clear/clarity

- o Leader provided no direction

- **Lack of Support**

- **Lack of Participation**

- **Lack of Trust**

- **Communication**

Q2. WAS THE ISSUE EVER RESOLVED?

Yes	No	Other
37%	80%	8%

When I see YES, I wonder how the issue was resolved and was it really resolved?

When I see NO at a whopping 80%, I think about the energy, productivity, time wasted, and ... profits lost. What's happening in organizations that we cannot resolve issues?

Q3. WHAT HAS BEEN YOUR BEST EXPERIENCE WITH A TEAM?

- Synergy

- Participation

- Team Support

- Ideas were executed, created, and contributed by all

- Combined talents

- Completed Project

- Leadership

    o   Leader valued each team member

    o   Servant leader

    o   Inspirational leader

    o   Available leader

Q4. HOW DID EITHER EVENT SHAPE YOUR THOUGHTS ABOUT TEAMS?

- "I prefer to lead now and am cautious when asked to join a team"

- "I prefer to work alone; independently"

- "Know who you are working with"

- "I do not like group work; I do not like teams"

- "Everyone does not give 100%"

- "I love working on teams with clear visions"

- "Working together helps"

- "It brings people together through engagement"

- "People need to be taught how to work together"

- "Teamwork is the only way to grow"

Q5. DEMOGRAPHICS

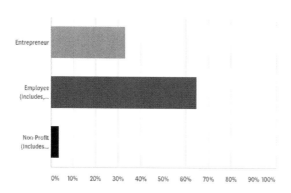

125 respondents

41 Entrepreneurs

80 Employees (corporate, government)

4 Non-profit (ministry, volunteer)

WHAT DID WE LEARN ?

The 2017 Pros and Cons of Teams Survey demonstrated that many organizations are stifled by their own internal dysfunction. Lack of clarity, leadership, and lack of accountability are all signs that team leaders and team members have not been developed to perform at a high vibration to create high-performance workplaces. Of course, there may be one or two rock stars on the team that get it and will perform exceptionally well regardless of what is occurring on the team, but can you imagine what would happen if everyone worked in sync, using their talents, skills, and abilities to perform at the highest level possible? It would be amazing, something to replicate in the organization, a productivity marker for excellence and surely we can't leave out the possible effect on profits when time is not wasted, and the "work" gets done.

There are two major issues preventing teams from being great, the first, being the battle of the BigE (big ego). In her book, EGO vs. EQ: How Top Leaders Beat 8 Ego Traps with Emotional Intelligence; Jen Shirkani discusses the eight ego traps that hold you back.

Ego Trap #1 Ignoring feedback you don't like: Shirkani says that executives and business owners need to ask themselves this question regularly: "How am I doing as a leader and how do I know I have an accurate answer?"

Ego Trap #2 Believing your technical skills are enough: This ego trap "gets triggered any time a leader overvalues his technical skills, industry knowledge, or field expertise at the expense of other emotionally intelligent leadership attributes, such as flexibility, self-control, and social skill," writes Shirkani.

Ego Trap #3 Only surrounding yourself with people like you: Shirkani states, "When you hire others who live on your wavelength, you unintentionally create a support system of people who are not equipped to challenge you, to question your thinking, or to offer you a different perspective and direction."

Ego Trap #4 Not yielding control: Just because you can do it, doesn't mean you should. Letting those tiny details go frees you up for more important tasks and creates a learning growth opportunity for someone else.

Ego Trap #5 Being blind to your downstream impact: "Shifting priorities arbitrarily, feeling hot about a project one day and cold the next, making everything a priority at once so that nothing is prioritized; All of these behaviors, and others, can get in the way of sustaining the organization's long-term goals and cloud the company's vision," says Shirkani.

Ego Trap #6 Underestimating how much you are being watched: John Maxwell says that people do what they see. When the Big E takes over, it can seriously affect the written and unwritten rules of the organization as well as the culture of the organization. Shirkani states, "Whether it's the time you arrive at work, the way you sign your emails, or the accolades you give or neglect to give to the team members at the year-end party in all these ways, and many more, your employees are watching you."

Ego Trap #7 Losing touch with the front-line experience: "As a senior executive, it is all too easy to become disconnected from the troops," writes Shirkani. "The contrast between the frontline environment and the physical surroundings of the average executive's private offices, dining-room-sized conference tables, and private gyms or private jets — is one reason."

Ego Trap #8 Relapsing back to your old ways: Remain consistent and authentic in all interactions with those in your organization. Being a flip-flopper will send the message that you are not genuine or trustworthy.

If you are on a team or leading a team, be sure you measure yourself by Shirkani's 8 Ego Traps and get your Big E (ego) in check.

The second is being chronically stuck in one of the stages of group/ team development; it's what Peter Lencioni describes in his book also titled, The Five Dysfunctions of a Team.

Team Dysfunction

The first area of dysfunction is the absence of trust. People are not willing to be vulnerable and speak honestly. The core of a cohesive team is trust and vulnerability. A team cannot thrive without it. One of the most effective ways to build trust in a team is our behavior and personality profiles. I will go into more detail on this in the next section.

The second area of dysfunction is fear of conflict. In this area, people will show up with what Lencioni calls "artificial harmony," not wanting to offend anyone and not being authentic. Once trust is established, a team then becomes unafraid to discuss and debate difficult issues.

The third area of dysfunction is lack of commitment. You can see from the survey responses that lack of commitment to a project will destroy a team. Ambiguity and having a "whatever" attitude affects the productivity and the morale of the team. Teams must buy in and commit to decisions despite initial disagreements.

The fourth area of dysfunction is lack of accountability. The survey yielded many results that spoke about people not pulling their weight, completing their part. On a team in any organization, there must be a willingness to call members out on their "stuff," being, behaviors that will harm the team, the project, the outcomes, and the goals. It is a necessary discomfort that will ultimately lead to the final dysfunction.

The final dysfunction, which is at the tip of the triangle is inattention to results. Herein lies a major problem because team members are focused on everything other than the project at hand. This can have a major impact on productivity and morale. This dysfunction is related to status and ego.

Lencioni's 5 team dysfunctions support the survey findings of why people give up on teams and prefer to work alone. In order to stop this dysfunction at the root, it's important for organizations to understand that results-driven teams are the secret sauce in an organization and they truly set the tone of the organizational culture.

Think about your first experience with a group project? A Team project? Think about how that experience shaped your thoughts about teams? Now think about how you show up on teams in your organization.

We've been conditioned to understanding that teams are the way to go, but deep down, that's probably the last thing we want to deal with. A team of people who don't think like me, work like me, and - heaven forbid - don't pull their own weight. Organizations fail at teams because they are made up of people who bring their bad experiences of being in a group or on a team into your organization, and it's affecting your productivity and your profits.

It's not their fault; they just haven't been developed and don't understand the power of a team! For a long time, I didn't either. Peter Lencioni said, *it's not finance, it's not strategy, and it's not technology. It is teamwork that remains the ultimate competitive advantage because it is so powerful and so rare.*

Teamwork IS the ultimate advantage when we understand its power! TEAMWORK isn't about just getting the job done, it's more about creating a culture. It took me 15 years to understand that there is an art to TEAMS because I was always a team of one. I had a collection of solo successes, and I loved it... until I got BUSHWACKED...

Starting my career early taught me how to win and that winning helped me to advance in my career really, fast. I can remember being promoted after 1 year because I had the best program outcomes in the state and they wanted to see if I could replicate that success. With this promotion came staff; WE WERE NOT a team. I was focused on designing the program, getting the numbers and winning.

That position took me to my Super Bowl! I was now a Statewide Coordinator, managing a budget of more than $25, 000, 000, and overseeing multiple programs across the state of Georgia. I had a government car, influence, perceived power, and I wwas under 30 years old. Yes! This was my career Super Bowl, and I created a lot of solo successes. I had collaborative partnerships, but I was still a solo team member. I had a solo-mindset.

And then I got BUSHWACKED...

After 15 years of playing hard and winning hard, I decided it was time for a change, and I transitioned into academia. The organization was impressed with my history and offered me a Department Chair position.

I was informed I would have a team of 20 staff members, with a few who were problematic. Although I knew I was going into a toxic culture, with problems, I was excited about how I would master the outcomes. It was horrible.

AND...

I failed!

 Funny thing, I thought I could do it all myself... When you are going into battle, you need an Army. You need a team.

Bill Gates said, "Success is a lousy teacher. It makes smart people think they can't lose" - I learned.

Whenever I fail, I ask myself three questions: what did I learn, what will I do, and what will I create.

What did I learn? No one does anything great alone, and I had not developed a team mindset.

What will   I do? I started studying everything about teams, competitive row boat teams specifically, and I got coached.

What will I create?

- A new mindset focusing on teams

- Teams in my business.

- I started helping my clients develop stronger teams because I could see their issues so much clearer.

- A result-driven philosophy for teams.

Teams are made up of people who drive policy, create processes, and influence productivity. This, in turn, will influence profits, customer service, and the overall health and culture of the organization.

Developing Power Teams for High Performing Organization begins with a strong, positive, and empowering culture. All organizations have a culture. It's either a positive or a negative culture. Culture is not to be confused with what you sell, how many widgets you make or what you develop. Culture is the core of who you are, who you choose to be, and how you show up inside and outside of the organization. The first step in creating results-driven teams is creating a culture where teams can thrive.

It doesn't matter how great you are as an individual, and it doesn't matter how many solo successes you've had. Can you complete the voyage by going at it alone? If your organization is built on having many people who have a history of solo success, they should be developed into high-performance power team leaders and members. Don't assume their past solo success, will lead to team successes because they won't. Thriving teams adopt, operate, and enforce covenants for high performing teams. I have outlined seven critical covenants for you to incorporate into your team culture.

ASSESS EVERYTHING AND DEVELOP EVERYONE

Assess everything and develop everyone. When I work with organizations, I like to complete a battery of assessments to determine where that organization is, where they want to go, and how much work we need to do to close the gap.

Assessment provides critical information by asking key questions: Who we are as an organization? Who are the people in this organization? How do they interact with each other? How can we improve? How to close the gaps between where you are and where you want to be.

When working with organizations, my team and I use a variety of assessments to obtain data, but these are the top three.

The first is an organizational assessment of people who sit in different levels in the organization, preferably not just the senior leadership. We look at what's actually happening organizationally using a game format based on The John Maxwell Leadership Game. It is a comprehensive game based on the teachings of John C. Maxwell. The game is fun and engaging, yet it challenges the participants to have open discussions to uncover gaps and areas for improvement within their organization. It helps organizations improve their leadership intelligence and increase their effectiveness. The qualitative data collected from this experience provides an amazing tool for individual and organizational development. When you develop together, you grow together.

The second assessment is an assessment that looks at the individual. Many assessments on the market look at the individual. The results tell you how great you are and the strengths you possess, but there are limits to those assessments because you begin to think singularly, which tends to create a posture that people should adjust to, who you are instead of using that assessment as a bridge.

It's important to understand who you are, most of us know that already, but it's more important to understand who you are in the context of working with others. The Wiley DiSC helps you do just that. The Wiley DiSC helps people at any level of an organization or industry effectively understand themselves and others. By establishing a common language that elevates the effectiveness of communication and teamwork, DiSC strengthens relationships which help improve productivity and lead to better workplaces. DiSC is a personality assessment based on a model of four basic styles: Dominance, Influence, Steadfastness, and Conscientiousness.

We all love working with people who get us, who think like us, who move like us, but again, that can be limiting and cause us to miss out on some key areas.

This level of assessment provides everyone with an opportunity to not only just look at who you are, which can be limiting, but better understand the qualities, skillset, and most importantly the value of others.

The final level of assessment is used to assist leaders and managers in gaining feedback on their blind spots, areas of growth, and leadership deficiencies. If you have always been in leadership positions like I was, or you always worked solo, you're not aware of your blind spots or the areas where you need to develop and grow.

John Maxwell calls it the Law of the Lid. You cannot grow your organization if you are not growing yourself. If you are not growing yourself, you cannot grow the team members. Your leadership ability determines the effectiveness of the growth of the organization. To grow up, you must raise your lid and the lid of those around you. You can only take people as far as you have been. For example, if your leadership ability is a 5, you can only take people to a 3. The 360 model allows you to gain feedback in an effective manner that facilitates growth. **The Wiley DiSC 363® for Leaders** combines the best of 360° feedback with the simplicity and power of DiSC, plus three strategies for improving leadership effectiveness.

Once the data has been collected, everyone will have the knowledge of areas for growth and expansion, who they are, and the simple shifts needed to create results-driven teams.

CREATE A TEAM MINDSET UPR VS CPR

Creating a team mindset starts with UPR, not CPR. Coming from a therapeutic counseling background, we're taught to always practice UPR unconditional positive regard, which means regardless of what the client says, the space is safe for them to speak their truth without fear, without judgment, and without retribution. However, many workplaces operate under CPR conditional positive regard, where it is not safe to speak your truth. Communication is guarded and people operate in fear of retribution. UPR doesn't mean that everyone will always agree or there won't be disagreements. It does mean that we will practice disagreeing without being disagreeable. All members and their ideas are valuable, and all voices will be heard. The leader must create a team mindset and a safe space for team members. When the culture of an organization supports this practice, it is easy for teams to perform at a higher frequency. This becomes an amazing incubator for building trust.

CREATE A COMMUNICATION STRUCTURE (CEUG)

There must be a strong communication structure when you're working with teams. There are four levels to this communication structure:

- Ensure that you have established a clear vision of the 3 W's. Where you're going, what you want, and why you are here. There must be at least 99.9% clarity before people leave the room. If you don't have all of the answers or you are not clear, do not form the team. When members leave the table with distorted clarity, it results in the "parking lot communication of strategy." This is when you're left to decipher what you thought you heard and it's usually always wrong. Eliminate the ball of confusion by establishing a clear vision. This doesn't mean all of the questions will have an answer, but most of them must.

- Identify the expectations. Members must know what is expected of them individually and collectively. A confident leader will ask the team what are your expectations of me? This becomes your paperless of flipchart contract of engagement.

- Stephen Covey said, "If I were to summarize in one sentence the single most important principle I have learned in the field of interpersonal relations, it would be this: Seek first to understand, then to be understood." To understand, you must LISTEN! A strong communication structure is 90% listening. It is effective at all levels of an organization and considered one of the most important life skills. Instead of creating an environment where everyone is vying to get their point across to be understood, create an environment focused on understanding. How do you create understanding through listening? Pay attention. Listen without interruption, judgment, or bias. Ask questions on the key points, provide feedback, respond to the facts of what is being said.

- Express gratitude. An article in Human Resources Today explored the findings of a study conducted by the Boston Consulting Group on appreciation versus compensation. "Over 200,000 global employees were studied by the Boston Consulting Group, and the top reason they reported enjoying their work was "feeling appreciated". The second, was having a good relationship with their supervisor; the fourth was that they had a good relationship with their colleagues. Financial compensation didn't appear until number 8! Four out of five employees (81%) say they are motivated to work harder when their boss shows appreciation for their work. Gratitude should be a part of the organizational core values. The leaders should ensure that every member feels valued and appreciated in the organization and for the work they provide to the team. Each member brings a unique quality, and it's a good feeling to be acknowledged for it. Gratitude should be expressed on an ongoing basis, not only during reviews but throughout the process. I love helping my clients come up with creative ways to show appreciation.

MANAGE ROADBLOCKS AND GIVE THEM SPACE TO CREATE AND UNDERSTAND THE STAGES OF DEVELOP- MENT

UPR and a great communication structure does not mean that working together means roasting marshmallows and singing rounds of 'Don't Worry Be Happy'. That's not realistic at all. For teams to perform at a high level, you must be vigilant for roadblocks to performance success. Understanding the stages of group/team development is key, but it is just as important for team leaders and the team members to understand how to avoid the rabbit hole and how not to stay in there too long. Sometimes taking a detour down the rabbit hole can provide great insight, however, put a time limit on it and the detour must be relevant to where you want to go. There will always be team members who are very passionate about where they stand in their ideas, but that passion should never create a roadblock to reaching the outcome.

Allow them to execute - provide space for them to create/fail/repair = Trust

Allow the team space to create, fail, and repair. This fosters trust between the team and the leader, the team and the organization and the team members. Whenever a group of people come together, there will be an opportunity for growth, success, and challenges, which are also known as failures. There is a risk, but there is a greater reward when we trust the process and the people we bring together.

Hold them accountable by monitoring, not micromanaging

Holding teams accountable is monitoring without micromanaging. Many of you will struggle with this because you have the desire to be in the middle of and have your hands on everything. It's not necessary. If you follow these steps, you will build the model of success. Now you have to let them do the work. It's your job to hold people accountable to what is expected by not interrupting or interceding upon the work that they have been tasked to do. Practice monitoring without micromanaging.

Rinse and Repeat throughout your organization

Bruce Eckfeldt, Contributor for Business Insider "It's not how hard you work, but how hard you work together" Results-driven teams work hard together.

©Glasbergen

"If we want to succeed as a team, we need to put aside our own selfish, individual interests and start doing things my way."

Results-Driven Customer Experience (Cx)

"The customer experience is the next competitive battleground."

-- Jerry Gregoire

Results-Driven Customer Experience (Cx)

Are you ready to have some fun? Well, of course, you are, because it's the holiday season! Well, it may not actually be the holiday season at the exact time that you are reading this book, but if it's not, I want you to imagine that it is.

This is a visioning exercise.

I want you to close your eyes and imagine it is your favorite holiday. I want you to think about everything that makes you happy and excited. What is it? Write it all down.

The holidays remind me of Results-Driven Customer Experiences because people display a willingness to SERVE. They go out of their way to create memorable experiences for young and old alike. That's what customer service is all about. Right? When I think about the efficiency and effectiveness of the holiday season, I think about what must occur to make the holiday a memorable experience for everyone involved.

You see, during the holidays, people are very giving. They give their time, their attention, and their knowledge, and it's done strategically for some and effortlessly for others.

If it's Mother's Day, people acknowledge you whether you are a mother or not. It's a universal display of courtesy and respect.

During Veterans Day, we show those who have risked their lives for our safety, gratitude and appreciation.

Even during Halloween, although I really don't get Halloween, it *RE-ALLY* does bring out the creativity in people! This is really what a customer experience is all about. Being willing to give, serve, and be creative while showing genuine courtesy and respect! The cherry on top is how we do it efficiently, effectively, effortlessly, and consistently throughout the organization.

Here's a question just to get you thinking.

Why can't we provide and maintain that same feeling and create those same experiences daily when we offer service to our internal and external customers?

Migs Bassig, a contributor for CustomerThink, a global online community of business leaders striving to create profitable customer-centric enterprises, serves 150,000 visitors from over 200 countries around the world, wrote an article, 5 Companies with Envy-Worthy Customer Experience.

Bassig researched and listed companies that were recognized as best-in-class, in terms of "putting customers first and managing their journeys". Bassig, determined, "these are the ones that are able to manage feedback effectively and wow customers consistently, resulting in higher customer satisfaction and loyalty, lower churn, increased revenue, and better overall business results. While the list is by no means an exhaustive one, we hope you'll be able to take what you can in order to inform and inspire your efforts to improve customer experience."

Bassig's article noted the following 5 companies:

- Zappos (retail, e-commerce) is a company known for going above and beyond to satisfy customers. They also have a School of WOW for inspiring leaders and frontline representatives with the Zappos customer service philosophy.

- Publix (retail, supermarket) based in Florida. The chain has a philosophy of building a people-first culture to share the customer experience. They were the only company with an overall rating of excellent in the 2015 and 2016 Temkin Experience Ratings.

- Southwest Airlines (airlines) is known for creating a moment of magic with customers. They were also the number 1 airline in the 2016 Temkin Experience Ratings.

- USAA (insurance and financial services) leverages technology to power customer experiences and foster trust; rated number 1 in 2016 Temkin Trust Ratings; Number 4 in 2016 Temkin Web Experience Ratings, number 1 in Forrester's U.S. 2016 Customer Experience Index, and number 1 in KPMG Nunwood's U.S. Customer Experience Excellence (CEE) rankings.

- Nordstrom (retail, department store) has a legacy of attention to detail when it comes to their customers. Their employee handbook concentrates on the company's "One Rule": "Use good judgment in all situations."

It's amazing that each of these 5 companies has made the customer experience an intentional priority. So why can't we do it in our organizations? What's stopping us from reaching stellar organizational success with our internal and external clients?

It's a culture. It's a belief system, and it's an inside job.

Stop and take a look at your organization's mission, vision, and core values.

Grab them now; I'll wait.

Please understand you cannot be efficient, effective, and maintain a healthy enterprise without creating a customer service experience no matter HOW HARD YOU TRY. It won't work!   There are certain behaviors that should be exhibited around efficiency and effectiveness that are directly related to a customer's experience.

So the question now becomes, what do you need to do, to truly do IT in order to be in compliance with who you are and the vision of your organization.

Now, Trust me!!

I know it's not easy. I worked for the State of Georgia for 10 years. I didn't get a raise for 5 years. I covered the entire state of Georgia without staff, but I created collaborative partnerships. I had to work with internal and external customers, politicians, and constituents. At times, it was challenging; you may not know this, but people have a certain perception of government workers. They think that they don't work enough, are lazy, and just another cog in the wheel of the bureaucratic system. To be honest with you, for some, those statements are true. I did not want that for myself.

So when I started my career, I was committed to providing excellence, and an experience that kept people coming back to me, which contributed to the organizational success. I was building a brand of customer service and didn't even know it. I didn't want to be like some of my colleagues. I wanted to be DIFFERENT! I wanted to be the "go-to get 'er done person," and I knew enough to know that it was easier to get what I wanted and needed if I went overboard to help my colleagues get what they needed. Zig Ziglar said it best, "you can have everything you want if you will just help others get what they want."

I was proud when people would call and say, "YOU answered your phone, WOW, you called me back on the same day, you rectified my problem, you helped me AND thanked you". People who were outside of my department would call me and ask for my help with things that were not my job, but I would help them too, if I could or if I knew the answer because I represented the Division, not just my job. We must break the "it's not my job" mentality.

The help that was needed generally didn't take any more time out of my day or take me away from what I needed to do, and I was happy to do it. Remember, I was building my brand... I was a credible, reputable source of information, and I never made them feel like they were bothering me. After all, I was a public servant.

Remember, it doesn't matter the organization serving, creating an experience will always reap a positive return.

- How are you serving?

- What example are you showing?

- What would your internal and external customers say about you?

People do business with people they know, like, and trust. Are you creating the know-like-trust factor with your internal and external customers?

Yes, I know it's difficult to think about customer service experience when you are being asked to do MORE with LESS. When you haven't received a salary increase in so many years, you have forgotten how long it's been, AND yet when there is still MORE work at the end of your day and LESS money at the end of your pay. In spite of all of that, I was personally committed to being different.

So TRUST ME, I UNDERSTAND, BUT as an individual and a representative of your organization, YOU MUST make a commitment to provide excellent customer service experiences, and you must execute customer service excellence DAILY!

Bill Gates said, "Every day we're saying, 'How can we keep this customer happy?' How can we get ahead in innovation by doing this because if we don't, somebody else will."

You see, it's a daily commitment because YOUR customer service is married to YOUR work ethic; I'm going to repeat that. It's a commitment because YOUR customer service is married to YOUR work ethic.

The way you provide service is a direct reflection of the credibility, and competence of you as an individual and the overall organization you represent. We all want to be seen as a credible source and as a competent individual in our area of expertise, but it's HOW we do it that adds that golden seal of service.

Customer service excellence is value plus or minus. You either add or subtract value when you are serving your customers. Adding value means you take ownership, and you make an effort to assist, resolve and deliver. Subtracting value means, you leave them frustrated, you have a "you're bothering me attitude," and you leave them with a negative impression of who you are as an individual and moreso the reflection it leaves on your organization.

A person may never remember your name, but they will always remember your organization. You want people to feel valued, and you want to add value to the people that you serve on a daily basis. You want them to look forward to interacting with you individually and collectively, but remember, it's a commitment, an operating system, the hard drive, and the platform for everything else that you do.

You may do information security very well.

You may do buildings and facilities very well.

You may do financial services very well.

You may do procurement and grants very well, BUT if your commitment to customer service is mediocre to poor, you need to reboot, you need a new hard drive, and a new operating system because poor service has a direct correlation to the root of your efficiency and effectiveness.

Sam Walton said, "The goal as a company is to have customer service that is not just the best, but legendary."

Think about these questions:

1. Are you contributing to legendary customer service?

2. How could you contribute to legendary service?

3. How can you model legendary service?

You are probably saying in a whiny voice, BUT you don't know my co-workers, you don't know the calls we receive, you don't know our customers, and how they challenge us, and you are right! I don't know... but I can only imagine. Remember, I was a public servant once. Nevertheless, there is still an expectation to provide a customer experience that gleams with excellence.

So, walk into the office tomorrow and say to a coworker, I will provide customer service excellence in spite of you AND in spite of ME or create a competition by seeing who can create the best customer experience for your internal and external clients. They may look at you odd. Just say you are setting your intention for the day and ask them to join you. I promise you, this will change how you do business as well as strengthen the culture of your organization.

Creating a customer experience is an inside job. It's a commitment. I have 9 tips to help you create an environment that caters to results-driven customer experiences in your organization.

COMMIT DAILY

Some of us have to work at it harder than others, and that's ok. Just commit to doing it. It's no different than an exercise plan, a productivity plan, or quitting smoking. Visualize yourself on the other end of that request or interaction and think about how you want to be treated or the outcome and then commit! Set your intention and remember "Everything starts with the customer" - Louis XIV

MANAGE THE TATT

Mehrabian's theory says, what we say accounts for 7% of our communication; The way we say it accounts for 38%, and what others see accounts for 55%

- Your temperament, defined as the combination of mental, physical, and emotional traits of a person; its natural predisposition and some people are naturally challenged with emotions.

- Your attitude – your attitude

- Your tone – how you sound when you say things

- Your tilt – your body language

LISTEN

We must become astute listeners. Many people hear to respond without truly practicing the art of listening. Why is listening important? People will request help or certain things from us that they really don't know how to verbalize. We need to listen closely so that we can ask clarifying questions in order to assist, serve, and direct. We become an investigator to help those who don't know what they don't know and don't know how to ask.

In David Ryback's book, *Putting Emotional Intelligence to Work*, there is a story about how Japanese managers worked to improve listening skills in the company for better productivity and effectiveness.

He goes on to state that during a plot, the managers were given 5 guidelines for better listening:

1. Maintain eye contact.

2. Don't cut off the other person's statements.

3. Respond genuinely.

4. Understand the process, not only the conclusions.

5. Don't impose your own view.

Just practicing those 5 steps alone will increase the customer service experience. Why, because depth listening causes you to go to the root, surface listening causes you to stay in the weeds.

Diversity

Managing your TATTs really comes in handy when you are working with people or in situations that are different from your comfort zone. If you are not comfortable with differences: racial, gender, sexual orientation, LGBTQ, elderly, and youth, you may struggle with being efficient and effective because you are no longer in your comfort zone.

I encourage you to be understanding and accepting of people or situations that are different from your familiar and outside of your comfort zone. Stephen Covey says, seek first to UNDERSTAND, then be UNDERSTOOD.

Be aware of your biases and your unconscious bias. Bias?

WHAT ARE UNCONSCIOUS BIASES?

Psychologists tell us that our unconscious biases are simply our natural people preferences. Biologically, we are hard-wired to prefer people who look like us, sound like us, and share our interests. Social psychologists call this phenomenon "social categorization" whereby we routinely and rapidly sort people into groups. This preference bypasses our normal, rational, and logical thinking. We use these processes very effectively (we call it intuition), but the categories we use to sort people are not logical, modern, or perhaps even legal. Put simply, our neurology takes us to the very brink of bias and poor decision making.

Neuro-psychologists tell us it is built into the very structure of the brain's neurons. Our unconscious brain processes and sifts vast amounts of information looking for patterns (200,000 times more information than the conscious mind). When the unconscious brain sees two things occurring together (e.g., many male senior managers), it begins to expect them to be seen together and starts to wire them together neurally.

Brain imaging scans have demonstrated that when people are shown images of faces that differ to from themselves, it activates an irrational prejudgment in the brain's alert system for danger; the amygdalae. This happens in less than a tenth of a second. Our associations and biases are likely to be activated every time we encounter a group member, even if we consciously think that we reject a group stereotype.

Unconscious bias operates at a very subtle level, below our awareness.

It results in almost unnoticeable behaviors, such as paying a little less attention to what the other person says, addressing them less warmly or talking less to them. We tend to be less empathetic towards people who are not like us. These behaviors are small, but could ultimately lead to long-term consequences that have a major impact on the effectiveness and efficiency of your organization.

EXAMPLES OF UNCONSCIOUS BIAS:

Unfortunately, we hear more stories of unconscious bias in the news almost daily. Here is a example:

Delta Airlines

When there was an emergency situation on her flight, Dr. Tamika Cross responded when the question was asked if a physician was onboard. To her surprise, she was met with "oh no, sweetie, put your hand down, we are looking for actual physicians or nurses or some type of medical personnel, we don't have time to talk to you." The call went out again for a physician, and Dr. Cross responded. This time being met with, "oh wow, you're an actual physician?" "let me see your credentials. What type of Doctor are you? Where do you work? Why were you in Detroit?" When a white male approached the situation, Dr. Cross was told, "thanks for your help, but he can help us, and he has his credentials."

Astonishing, right? A man's life was in jeopardy and someone's bias getting in the way could have meant life or death. Organizations cannot afford to ignore bias of any kind. It must be addressed and monitored before an occurrence. Unconscious bias must be discussed and addressed in every organization and at all levels because it has a tremendous effect on the internal and external customer experience. Delta Airlines, Starbucks, Waffle House... today, tomorrow it could be you and your organization.

Be FAT, Flexible, Adaptable, and Teachable. It is in these moments that we increase our awareness, of how we can best serve and learn.

OWNERSHIP

Ownership is about follow up and follow through, making sure you have another satisfied customer and another productive meeting. That might mean assisting them with navigation. Provide high-quality services and solutions that are timely, accurate, and meet the overall vision and mission.

CONFIDENT

Do not use passive language. Examples: I think, I guess or it might. Be confident in the information you are providing OR be confident in your ability to find the answer. Passive language sends a direct message that you either don't want to help me or participate OR you don't know how... This leads to #7.

CREDIBLE AND COMPETENT

Customer service excellence is about credibility and competence. Credibility is defined as being capable of persuading people that something will happen or be successful. You gain this designation of being a credible source from your demonstrated past behavior and experiences. Competence is defined as having the necessary ability, knowledge, or skill to execute something successfully (execute is an action word).

Credibility is about TRUST and Competence is KNOW HOW! Know your 3 Knows.

Know your information.

Know your limits.

Know who to ask.

Being competent doesn't mean you have to have all the answers. You can be a rock star just because you know who to ask for the answer. Instead of saying that's not my job, not my department, I don't know, or just not responding at all; seek opportunities to serve instead of sending the message, IT'S NOT MY PROBLEM.

When people trust you and KNOW that you KNOW how to get things done, it creates a win-win-win.

MENTAL STATUS CHECK

If I asked you what happened when you left work yesterday, I'm sure I would hear a lot of things that could have an impact on your effectiveness and definitely your service. There are so many things that can happen between the time we leave work and arrive back to work. Examples: sick babies, flat tires, dealing with aging parents, marital discord, continuing education, children's homework, your dog died.

Add your own examples. Life happens and your internal and external customers don't know or care about the happenings of your life, when they are trying to work with you. You need to make it a practice to do a mental status check to make sure that the events of the evening before don't track in to work with you the next day like "poo on your shoe." Remember point number one is to commit daily and to leave all issues that do not pertain to work on the doormat outside.

ASSESSMENT

Assess yourself to see how you did each week. See if you've grown, if you've adjusted, and how it's helped you, your team, and the people you serve. You may see a huge improvement in how people respond to you. You may find that your influence has increased. You may even find that you have become more effective and efficient, and when all three are aligned, it makes for a high performance organization.

Remember, if you focus on creating customer experiences that cater to your customers' wants and desires, build long-term relationships, and service your customers far beyond the level of service that your competition would provide, your organization will flourish. You may charge higher rates, and your customers will gladly support you. All your profits depend on your customers.

Do you know what your internal and external customers want?

©Glasbergen
glasbergen.com

"Good customer service is rare. When something is
rare, it is valuable. When something is valuable,
it is expensive. Bad customer service is our
way of helping our customers save money!"

Results-Driven Execution (The Work)

Without execution, 'vision' is just another word for hallucination

-- *Mark Hurd*

Results-Driven Execution (The Work)

I am the Queen of Execution. I am writing this chapter while on a cruise ship in the middle of the ocean, and I'm dreaming about execution. I wake up in the middle of the night and make notes about things I want to execute. I write ideas of things to execute on napkins, but when it came to writing this chapter I struggled, procrastinated and delayed. Just like many of you when it comes to implementation. Something else takes priority, you get waylaid by something more important, it's not the right time, you can't focus or my favorite, you are uninspired. All reasons that keep you from executing.

I assumed writing this chapter would be the easiest because I spend a large part of my time helping organizations with implementation and execution, which is what I love most.

I didn't want to be like people who are geniuses at math, but don't teach it well. They can leave their students feeling overwhelmed and confused. Execution is the critical element to organizational success. Putting the pedal to the medal for execution requires a blueprint of clarity, strategy, teams, accountability, action, and a lot of movement. You can not execute standing still or mulling over things until the next fiscal year. The time is now to take action! Many organizations develop wonderful strategic plans and stop dead in their tracks instead of moving forward with implementation. You develop your strategic plan to the final degree but you never push the go button for execution. Therein lies the problem. It is only through execution that you can begin to design the organizational success you envision. You must put feet on your vision in order for them to run toward organizational success. Without execution, it will only remain a plan or yet another dream deferred. Just another idea and ideas are cheap. Ideas are easy. Ideas are common. Everybody has ideas. Ideas are highly overvalued. Execution is all that matters, said Casey Neistat.

In order to execute, you must do a few things, or in this instance, stop doing things that cause execution to halt. When you remove the barriers, it makes execution a lot easier. Make a commitment to stop doing those things that continue to hold you and your organization hostage and keep you stuck. This behavior keeps you in the cycle of ego, blame, would have, could have, and let's not forget, should have.

So let's get started with a few stops to prepare for an execution mindset.

1. Stop making excuses and procrastinating. Excuses and procrastination are partners in crime and they work against all of your organizational goals. Write down each excuse that is standing in the way of your organizational growth. This requires a lot of honesty. Then make a list of why you are blaming, shaming, making excuses, and procrastinating. This also requires honesty, and it may cause you to make some adjustments to your strategic plan. Remember, excuses and procrastination are partners in crime, and they work together to keep you from moving and executing.

2. Stop being negative. Unfortunately, many leaders learn to lead from past leaders who carried a big stick of negativity. This spreads like wildfire in your organization. Being negative will

keep you from executing your organizational plan. Ask some-one you trust how many negative statements you make a day, a week, as it relates to your organization, the team, and the progress? You could be stopping the growth by the words you use.

Once you get your feedback, commit to turning your words into positive statements of affirmation. Negative energy does not produce positive outcomes. Focus on your cans and not your cant's. Negative energy keeps you and your organization stuck. Replace negative statements with positive affirmations about your project, your team and your ability to lead.

3. Stop wasting your energy on things that do not concern you. It's easy to delay your own execution when you are busy meddling and stirring the pot of things that don't matter. Everything is not about you nor does it require your involvement. It does require that you let it go. Be the example you want to see in your organization. Stay focused on the plan, get back into your lane and execute! How much time are you devoting to someone or something else that could be redirected to organizational execution?

4. Stop letting fear control your steps. The F-word causes angst for many people. Designing the strategy is easy, but fear is the paralyzing factor that keeps you stuck. There are many situations that cause nervousness and anxiety but you cannot allow those feelings to keep you bound. You cannot have faith and fear at the same time. You must learn to reconfigure fear and use it as motivation and energy to conquer those things you desire in your organization and for your team. Reconfigure fear and use it as powerful petroleum that will motivate you to MOVE you and your organization to success!

5.   Stop beating yourself up on past mistakes. Been there, done that? What's keeping you from doing it again? Oh, you are perfect, huh? You aren't supposed to make mistakes, huh? Really? John Maxwell says, sometimes you win, and sometimes you learn. What did you learn? Executing does not mean that the plan is going to result in a perfect outcome, and guess what, we might just bomb totally and that is just fine. It is an opportunity to revisit the plan, adjust, and execute again. Think about your favorite sports team. When they lose, they go back, watch the plays, redesign the plays and come back stronger than ever. We all learn from our mistakes. Do not allow mistakes to keep you on the bench and out of the game. This is the game of execution, get back in there!

6.   Stop waiting and competing with others. I'm waiting on Sue. I'm waiting on Joe. Guess what, they are waiting on you too. Stop the competition mindset and realize that these are your organizational goals. The reality is, if you are waiting on someone to tell you it's a great idea, you should do it, I'm behind you 100%, forget about it! It's not going to happen. Chances are, those people won't make statements like that UNTIL they see you execute.

7.   Stop spending time with energy zappers. When you are on a mission for creating a high performance workplace, you must not be deterred by the naysayers. They will ZAP your energy. They are what kryptonite is to Superman. You know who and what they are, create an exit strategy and exit stage left while you are in the execution phase. Find a place for them so they can use their skillset in a productive manner.

8.   Tomorrow, tomorrow, I love ya tomorrow, you're only a day away, says the famous song from the Broadway show, Annie. The truth of the matter is, tomorrow is more than a day away

because there is always another tomorrow to delay what needs to be done today. Do it today, do it NOW. Do it shaking in your boots if you must, but do it! Stop deferring the vision for organization excellence.

These are my top tips for executing your way to organizational success and while creating a high performance workplace. Once you master these tips, you must begin to model them for others on your team. Leaders create more leaders by using their influence for growth. You now have the tools to create a results-driven organization and develop high performers in critical areas to your organization. Don't let this be yet another vacuum of information that you consume. Get into action and start today.

©Glasbergen
glasbergen.com

"I want you to find a bold and innovative
new way to do everything exactly the same
way we've been doing it for 25 years."

APPENDIX

RESULTS DRIVEN STRATEGIC PLANNING RESOURCE GLOSSARY

Resource Planning: Before the Strategic plan can be finally agreed and implemented, the leader(s) must ensure that there will be sufficient resources available for each activity at each stage of the plan. In reality the planning for the provision of resources must be viewed as a critical element of the plan itself. The strategic plan and the objectives within it will not be achieved if the activities needed to carry out the plan are not properly supported by appropriate resources.

Resources Forecast: A resources forecast should be carried out. All planned activities, stages, and objectives, should be analyzed for resource requirements (resources as in the list below). If the forecast identifies areas where the available or deliverable resources do not match the levels required, then this must be corrected or the plan must be altered. Once the leader(s) can be satisfied that the necessary resources will be available, the plan can be finalized and implemented with confidence.

Prioritizing Resources: It is tempting to rank these resources, perhaps arguing that human resources, and accompanying expertise and experience should be the highest on the list, but this is not logical. Lack of, or inadequate, financial, physical, or systems resources for any one of the many activities, or at any stage of the plan, can be as damaging as not having the required human resources. It is also tempting to think of resources as only human, financial, or physical, and also as coming only from internal sources. Again, this is not appropriate, as the strategic plan needs support from other areas, internally and externally, that should also be described as resources, such as systems, policies, suppliers, external stakeholders.

Organizational Infrastructure: The shape and complexity of the organizational structure should be designed to serve the strategic direction taken. A structure that is as flexible, dynamic, and responsive a structure as possible is essential. In some business sectors, for example in many parts of the public sector, there will be constraints and barriers that will dictate a more bureaucratic and rigid structure that limits responsiveness and flexibility. Much of this may be unavoidable, but it should be continually challenged and loosened where possible. In most other sectors there is no excuse. The leaders of organizations in commercially driven sectors, and this now includes education, health, charities, and the utilities, must strive to structure their organizations so that they can respond to the fast pace and continual changes of today's business world.

Systems, Policies, Procedures: In functional areas such as IT, Finance, HR and Personnel, Performance Appraisal and Reward, Conditions of Employment, Working Patterns, Training and Development, the systems, policies, and procedures must be operating in support of the strategic plan and the accompanying operational activities. An appropriate Quality Assurance Management System should be in place, guided by the strategic objectives, constantly monitoring the quality standards of all the systems, including its own, to ensure that they are not hindering or damaging the chances of achieving the strategic objectives.

Location: For most organizations the location is not easily changeable, and would not normally be challenged. But the leader(s) must look at the current location in terms of its strategic suitability. If the location is not supportive to the strategies, then alternatives must at least be explored. If moving to a more appropriate location is logistically and financially possible, then that relocation should take place at the earliest opportunity.

Front-line Physical Resources: For manufacturing organizations this will encompass production facilities, plant, equipment, and so on. For service sector organizations this will mean the physical resources at the point of sale and-or delivery points. The condition and capacity of physical resources in these areas must be able to meet the operational demands dictated by the strategies.

Support Functions Physical Resources: For most organizations this means activity areas such as procurement, design, research and development, administration, finance, human resources, maintenance, marketing, sales, distribution, and so on.

Managers in front-line and support areas must focus on achieving the operational objectives that have been derived from the strategic plans. The leader(s) must implement a system of regular performance appraisal and consultation to ensure that these areas are resourced appropriately and operated effectively.

Suppliers: A key resource, but because they are outside the organization, are often forgotten. The quality of supplies, be they raw materials, equipment, parts, consumables, people, or advisory services, is a critical factor in the capability of the organization. If inputs are not of the right quality then costs can rise, damage can be caused, delays can occur, and the operational performance of the organization could suffer. In turn, the achievement of the strategic objectives of the organization could be delayed or damaged.

Human Resources: The question that the leader(s) must ask is whether the quality, quantity, and distribution of the human resources within the organization, is sufficient to satisfy the needs of the chosen strategies. Existing staffing levels, degrees of expertise and experience, flexibility, distribution, predicted wastage or turnover, are all areas that need analyzing. Intangible factors, such as levels of morale, motivation, cultural attitudes, should also be evaluated. A human resources audit must be carried out and where gaps or weaknesses are identified these must be corrected, and brought up to the required levels.

Financial Resources: In simple terms, the leader(s) must be satisfied that the funding, the cash-flows, the budgets, will meet the demands of the activities. If necessary, and affordable, additional funding must be obtained, linking this resource need to external stakeholders as discussed below, such as banks, shareholders, and other investors.

Marketing and Distribution: whatever the product or service that the organization is offering, the marketing and distribution functions are as important, if not more so, than any other internal function. Without revenue, whether from customer sales, grants, government funds, or other sources, the organization must persuade the purchaser, or provider, to deliver revenue to it. This revenue will be a critical element of the financial resources needed to support the planned activity, and the continued flow of this revenue must be protected. This entails ensuring that the marketing and distribution function is itself appropriately funded.

External Stakeholders: This group of resource sources includes shareholders, investors and other funding organizations discussed in the section on Financial Resources. These need to be managed and informed appropriately. Other stakeholders could, depending on the nature of the business, include the local authorities, public services, local and-or national media, trade unions, local residents, national or   international governments, national   or international trade organizations, business partners, and so on. Where the support of any external stakeholder is identified as important to the success of the strategic plan, then effort and energy should be spent on building and maintaining a positive relationship with them. Maintaining positive relationships with external stakeholders is essential, as they are a vital resource in supporting the organization's strategic direction.

Intangible Resources: These include goodwill, reputation, and brands. Individually and collectively these can be important to the success of the strategic plan. Goodwill is a value given to the reputation, the customer loyalty, the brand values, and in some cases the public image of the organization. In monetary terms it is the difference in saleable value, or total value, between the tangible assets value given to the business and the actual value that a buyer would pay or an investor would calculate when deciding to invest or not. Reputation that the organization has amongst its competitors, with its customers, in the public psyche, and although difficult to calculate, is also valuable. Brands can be highly valuable, as demonstrated by some of the best known, which generate immediate positive responses throughout the world. These intangible assets are resources, with a value, which the strategic plan will have considered and made use of, or planned to protect, or develop, as part of the plan. The leader(s) must ensure that these resources, these assets, are managed effectively and support the strategic plan as intended.

Management: The effectiveness of the individuals and teams that make up the management of the organization are critical to the success of the chosen strategies. Without an effective management network supporting the planned activity and striving to achieve the strategic and operational objectives, the strategies will fail. As discussed in an earlier article, the leader(s) must put in place an effective management network, and ensure that this highly valuable resource is itself resourced appropriately.

The Operational Employees: Sadly this resource, this group of people, is often overlooked when the achievement of strategic objectives is discussed. Wrongly, it is assumed that objectives can be achieved if there is good management, good leadership, and appropriate financial and physical resources in place. Not true. Unless the workforce is appropriately skilled, experienced, qualified, continuously developed, and committed to support the achievement of the strategic plans, then the plans will fail. It is critical that the operational employees, in all functional areas, are involved, informed, and persuaded to support the strategic plan. The role of the leader(s) here is to ensure that the management team makes this happen.

Leadership: The final resource that we look at is the leadership of the organization. The role of the leader(s) is to lead the organization into the future, in a direction and a condition that will ensure that the organization is successful. Whichever direction is chosen and whatever the measure of success is, the leader(s) must make certain that the strategic plan is appropriately resourced at every stage and in every activity area. In addition, the leader(s) must ensure that they lead the organization in an appropriate manner, adopting an appropriate style of leadership for each stage of the journey that the strategic plan is leading the organization into.

The leader(s) must ensure that the plan is resourced appropriately and then accept responsibility for being the most critical resource of all. Without the essential resource of effective leadership, regardless of how well other resources are provided and applied, the plans will fail.

RESULTS DRIVEN LEADERSHIP CHECKLIST

CHARACTERISTICS OF A RESULTS DRIVEN LEADER

- Results Driven Leaders are learners – Results Driven Leaders are constantly learning new and innovative ways of doing things. That also means leaders are open to constructive criticism and changing harmful habits.

- Creates momentum – A Results Driven Leader must be moving forward at all times. When you create momentum in yourself and your team, you head people who are poised to reach the finish line to success.

- Impeccable ethics and morals – When you apply ethical and moral standards to your methods of leadership, you'll respect others' rights and dignity. Those you lead will also develop ethical and moral standards.

- Ability to communicate – You can't present yourself as a Results Driven Leader unless you know how to communicate well with others. Communication is a two-way street – people must hear and understand you before you can communicate your views.

- Magnet to others – If you want to attract and lead others, become the person who appeals to them through actions, visions and viewpoints. Like-minded people are naturally attracted to each other, so if you project the type of person you want to attract, you'll have a successful team.

- Be accountable – Results Driven Leaders take responsibility for every action you choose and every choice you make. The old saying, "The buck stops here," is true for all leaders, whether you're the coach of a team or the president of a company.

- Encourage creativity – When you're leading a group, always encourage your members of the team to spread their wings and become a creative contributor.

- Results Driven Leaders have a profound interest in others – Part of becoming a great communicator and being able to lead others means that you must be interested in what other people are all about. Even the person you perceive to be uninteresting might surprise you and teach you something.

- Results Driven Leaders knows how to prioritize – To complete any worthwhile venture, it's important to prioritize and set goals. Without goal setting, projects aren't completed satisfactorily, if at all, and chaos is bound to occur.

THE 10 KEYS OF RESULTS DRIVEN LEADERSHIP

1. Establish a Framework of Trust - Without the trust of others, you fail as a leader.

2. Be Genuine - Unless you're genuine and sincere in actions and words, others will doubt you.

3. Demonstrate Integrity - Without integrity, success means nothing. Dwight Eisenhower, former Army general during World War II and later, President of the United States, once said, "The supreme quality for leadership is unquestionably integrity."

4. Display Loyalty - When you're loyal to something or someone, you become faithful to it and all that it stands for.

5. Create a Culture for Positive Change - Whether you're leading an organization or a family, creating positive change within is a true sign of leadership.

6. Develop Intuition - You've probably had people tell you to "trust your gut," when faced with an issue which could go either way. But, what if you don't trust your instincts to lead you down the right path – especially if it hinges on an important issue or life change?

7. Develop Relationships - Unless you learn the art of truly connecting with others, becoming a leader will evade you.

8. Have a Shared Vision - From George Washington to modern day leaders – each had a vision they worked and dwelled on until it became reality.

9. Create Momentum - Successful leaders know how to create momentum that will help things move continuously forward to the end goal.

10. Attitude is everything - Can you gauge how your attitude is affecting others? It's the mark of true leadership to be able to see the impact their current attitude is having on those around them.

2017 PROS AND CONS OF TEAM SURVEY RESULTS

Q1 WHAT WAS YOUR WORST EXPERIENCE WITH A TEAM?

Answered: 125   Skipped: 0

#	RESPONSES	DATE
1	Team players not pulling their weight.	11/21/2017 2:19 PM
2	I disruptive member who was hostile and threaten team members	11/16/2017 12:28 PM
3	Everyone on a team is not really on the team or a team player. Because you wear the shirt didn't mean a thing.	11/13/2017 6:42 AM
4	When members do not cooperate. When there is a lack of respect for the overall vision of seeing the project through as the vision it is intended to be. Basically everyone is not in it for the success of the operation.	11/13/2017 5:34 AM
5	No support	11/12/2017 2:24 PM
6	Everyone not cooperating to get the task done	11/10/2017 1:55 PM
7	Having 1 or more people fail to adequately do their part.	11/10/2017 1:02 PM
8	Slackers	11/10/2017 10:39 AM
9	Unresolved disagreements due to personality differences	11/10/2017 8:51 AM
10	No participation	11/10/2017 8:31 AM
11	When one person decided they were not going to complete the assignment as instructed. It was very obvious when we presented	11/10/2017 7:58 AM

12	Those who want to take over and not work as a team but show how smart they are as an individual.	11/10/2017 7:45 AM
13	During grad school when people on the team would not pull their weight and help with the work.	11/10/2017 7:44 AM
14	Having to pick up the slack of others at the last minute.	11/10/2017 7:41 AM
15	Everyone not pulling equal weight	11/10/2017 7:39 AM
16	No voice	11/10/2017 7:37 AM
17	Working with a team that didn't want to collaborate which makes being part of a teaching team extremely tough.	11/10/2017 7:06 AM
18	When the Team Leader does nothing but is given or takes all the credit	11/10/2017 7:04 AM
19	Team members that refuse to work.	11/10/2017 6:26 AM
20	Everyone doesn't have the team mindset	11/10/2017 6:24 AM
21	When a new team mate comes in and tries to sabotage a cohesive established team.	11/10/2017 6:19 AM
22	Being on a team where no one else wanted to do the work assigned	11/10/2017 6:15 AM
23	Feeling like I was in competition with my team mates. There was not true collaboration. Person won an award for work that was basically my own and no acknowledgment that I provided the support to pull the project through.	11/10/2017 6:15 AM
24	Members of the team not doing their fair share of the work.	11/10/2017 6:14 AM
25	People not doing their part	11/10/2017 6:01 AM
26	Losing	11/10/2017 5:59 AM
27	Team quitting	11/10/2017 5:54 AM
28	Not feeling that the work being given by partners was at my caliber of academic/ work ethic.	11/10/2017 1:44 AM
29	Inequality	11/10/2017 1:37 AM
30	Not completing task or not coming to presentation	11/10/2017 12:51 AM

31	Non compliance	11/10/2017 12:19 AM
32	Others not followed through on their part of the assignment	11/10/2017 12:18 AM
33	Lack of Team effort by all	11/10/2017 12:05 AM
34	One professional taking over everyone's role, offering advice outside of their scope of practice	11/9/2017 11:46 PM
35	Afraid to lead or take responsibility	11/9/2017 11:43 PM
36	Lack of communication and trust. Lastly, lack of sharing pertinent knowledge.	11/9/2017 11:25 PM
37	Everyone not putting in the same amount of effort	11/9/2017 11:18 PM
38	Change is difficult when you are seen as the outsider.	11/9/2017 11:01 PM
39	People who think they know it all or on the flip side people who didn't know what they were doing, had a bad attitude and didn't pull their weight	11/9/2017 10:51 PM
40	People not pulling their weight.	11/9/2017 10:47 PM
41	Everyone not participating	11/9/2017 10:11 PM
42	I'm the only one working	11/9/2017 9:56 PM
43	When my participation was ignored or not valued	11/9/2017 9:48 PM
44	When all members do not participate equally and some at all but takes the credit because they're 'on the team'.	11/9/2017 9:32 PM
45	All people not doing their part	11/9/2017 9:29 PM
46	Compensating for the team Slackers	11/9/2017 9:21 PM
47	Failure of other members to perform. I ended up doing most of the project myself so we would not fail.	11/9/2017 9:12 PM
48	Leaders that do not work	11/9/2017 9:01 PM
49	Leader not showing examples	11/9/2017 8:56 PM
50	Non-participation	11/9/2017 8:55 PM

51	Working in a volunteer organization with a group of people who 1) were cliquish 2) the officers had extremely poor leadership ski 3) other team members were clueless about how to conduct business 4) some of the members had questionable integrity 5) many members resented me for speaking up and insisting we work according to mandated guidelines, and then I was verbally attacked for calling out inappropriate behavior.	11/9/2017 8:53 PM
52	Team with a poor leader	11/9/2017 8:41 PM
53	People who aren't team players and want all the credit	11/9/2017 7:52 PM
54	When you have one person who want to run the show.	11/9/2017 7:13 PM
55	A leader who didn't listen	11/9/2017 7:12 PM
56	People leaving me to do all the work	11/9/2017 6:05 PM
57	The team didn't patronize each other	11/9/2017 6:04 PM
58	Team members not pulling their weight.	11/9/2017 5:56 PM
59	Members not pulling their weight	11/9/2017 5:39 PM
60	Working with aggressive, unprofessional people	11/9/2017 5:16 PM
61	A work related subcommittee	11/9/2017 5:11 PM
62	One person doing all the work	11/9/2017 5:10 PM
63	College group assignments	11/9/2017 5:07 PM
64	A bad boss	11/9/2017 5:02 PM
65	Non participatory members	11/9/2017 5:00 PM
66	Leader of the team pitting the team against one another	11/9/2017 4:59 PM
67	Getting stuck with all the work	11/9/2017 4:46 PM

68	Not being able to voice my opinion	11/9/2017 4:44 PM
69	Team members afraid to address a rude out of line member	11/9/2017 4:40 PM
70	Even though there is no I in team, most do see the ME in team, and it is all about them. They commit to the team, then get busy, forget, the list goes on - this covers job, church, direct sales, entrepreneurial start-up team, again ... the list goes on.	11/9/2017 4:39 PM
71	Lack of communication	11/9/2017 4:33 PM
72	Noncontributing team members	11/9/2017 4:32 PM
73	Restating the problem instead of finding ways to solve it.	11/9/2017 4:27 PM
74	On the job, when a team member failed to show up and do her assigned duties.	11/9/2017 4:25 PM
75	One with poor leadership...frustrating	11/9/2017 4:18 PM
76	A domineering senior member who intimidated other staff members.	11/9/2017 4:12 PM
77	When people don't do what they said they would do and the team does not accomplish its goal.	11/9/2017 3:56 PM
78	Individuals who do not pull their weight, and superfluous group texts.	11/9/2017 3:53 PM
79	Jealousy	11/9/2017 3:38 PM
80	One or more team members not pulling their weight	11/9/2017 3:18 PM
81	Folks who do nothing or do not "own their part".	11/9/2017 2:31 PM
82	Cliques	11/9/2017 1:52 PM
83	Haven't had a bad experience working with a team so far.	11/9/2017 1:11 PM

84	Working with people who are selfish	11/9/2017 1:01 PM
85	Having a non-contributor on the team...The person just did not do their portion or any portion of the task to be completed.	11/9/2017 12:03 PM
86	Non participation	11/9/2017 12:03 PM
87	Buena hay de todo	11/9/2017 11:26 AM
88	Laggers. People who do not pull their weight.	11/9/2017 10:43 AM
89	My worst experience(s) have been: No clear mission with clear assignments. Buy into the mission energizes everyone.	11/9/2017 10:28 AM
90	Everyone not being on the same page and doing their part.	11/9/2017 10:27 AM
91	Everyone think he/she knows what is best for the team	11/9/2017 10:19 AM
92	Not being heard and someone else says the same thing you said and they get praised11/9/2017 10:08 AM	
93	Master program Virtual team project to complete our paper for class. It's tougher teaming online with those you've never met, you can't pick up the phone and Call, and everything is done in a team room environment, and you have team members who don't do their part of the assignment, or half does it. One team member didn't do theirs and would not communicate. We had to complete her part at the last minute. She got upset when we didn't want her to get credit for the paper. We reported to the teacher online the situation. She got credit anyway.	11/9/2017 6:36 AM
94	Betrayal	11/9/2017 12:34 AM
95	Someone taking credit for all or more than their share of the work. Someone not doing their fair share,	11/8/2017 11:50 PM
96	Being on firing squad. Being told by everyone what they did not like me	11/8/2017 8:51 PM
97	People that don't share.	11/8/2017 7:46 PM

98	A coworker that tried to sabotage the work of her coworkers by omitting information needed for a project.	11/8/2017 7:45 PM
99	I don't understand this question as it is worded	11/8/2017 5:38 PM
100	Distance and not feeling connected	11/8/2017 12:19 PM
101	Not consistent	11/8/2017 11:17 AM
102	Having group projects not submitted and completed on time. This in turn effected my overall grade.	11/8/2017 11:13 AM
103	Different personalities clashing	11/8/2017 10:48 AM
104	I have several, people have stolen my ideas and passed them off as their own. They have also made me do all of the work bring the project to a close	11/8/2017 10:38 AM
105	The other person not pulling their weight	11/8/2017 10:25 AM
106	Having to do the task a team would not do.	11/8/2017 10:17 AM
107	Inconsistency	11/8/2017 10:16 AM
108	Everyone didn't pull their own weight	11/8/2017 9:54 AM
109	Procrastination on the part of another team member and then not having the time to correct mistakes or improve the content.	11/8/2017 9:51 AM
110	Being accused of not participating on the team's idea by someone who was minimize the efforts of others to garner attention.	11/8/2017 9:48 AM
111	Lack of trust that others will work as hard as they do.	11/8/2017 9:27 AM
112	Lack of balance on level of participation	11/8/2017 8:39 AM
113	Teamwork	11/8/2017 8:14 AM
114	When egos over-ride the collective agenda	11/8/2017 7:58 AM

115	People...lol only half kidding but those who were not fully invested. Are always a problem	11/8/2017 7:27 AM
116	Teams where everyone is only looking out for themselves.	11/8/2017 6:29 AM
117	Not organized	11/8/2017 5:16 AM
118	Lack of community & communication	11/8/2017 12:54 AM
119	In high school basketball we lost nearly every game. In a work environment, mostly if we argued a lot, or spent too much time planning and not doing things.	11/8/2017 12:53 AM
120	People not living up to expectations	11/8/2017 12:24 AM
121	Doing all of the work but sharing the credit.	11/8/2017 12:08 AM
122	Incompetence	11/7/2017 10:58 PM
123	Sabotage from team member	11/7/2017 10:57 PM
124	My worst experience with a team was with a mental health team and the lead was not pulling her weight.	11/7/2017 10:52 PM
125	When I had to do everything	11/7/2017 10:43 PM

Q2 WAS THE ISSUE EVER RESOLVED?

Answered: 125   Skipped: 0

#	RESPONSES	DATE
1	No.	11/21/2017 2:19 PM
2	She was removed from the project.	11/16/2017 12:28 PM
3	No	11/13/2017 6:42 AM
4	Yes, sometimes it is a very slow process. Depending on the willingness of others to cooperate, or the removal of those who lack sharing the same vision of success for the overall team.	11/13/2017 5:34 AM
5	No, were selfish	11/12/2017 2:24 PM
6	Yes	11/10/2017 1:55 PM
7	No	11/10/2017 1:02 PM
8	No	11/10/2017 10:39 AM
9	No	11/10/2017 8:51 AM
10	No	11/10/2017 8:31 AM
11	The instructor was notified and she stated that she was aware and her grade would be in jeopardy	11/10/2017 7:58 AM
12	Yes and no. Yes because we still had to get the project done as a group, but no because that individual still wanted to boss everyone.	11/10/2017 7:45 AM
13	No not really, but the work got done.	11/10/2017 7:44 AM
14	No	11/10/2017 7:41 AM
15	Yes but not in a positive way.	11/10/2017 7:39 AM

16	No	11/10/2017 7:37 AM
17	No, and the school year presented many challenges.	11/10/2017 7:06 AM
18	No	11/10/2017 7:04 AM
19	No	11/10/2017 6:26 AM
20	No	11/10/2017 6:24 AM
21	It's a recent issue and she continues to sometimes isolate herself from the team. No, the issue is not resolved.	11/10/2017 6:19 AM
22	No, I did the work myself	11/10/2017 6:15 AM
23	No!	11/10/2017 6:15 AM
24	Yes, once it was addressed.	11/10/2017 6:14 AM
25	Yes	11/10/2017 6:01 AM
26	Yes	11/10/2017 5:59 AM
27	No	11/10/2017 5:54 AM
28	Not in that group. Prereqs are now given when working with others	11/10/2017 1:44 AM
29	No	11/10/2017 1:37 AM
30	Yes	11/10/2017 12:51 AM
31	Yes	11/10/2017 12:19 AM
32	No, others filled in to get the job done	11/10/2017 12:18 AM
34	No,	11/9/2017 11:46 PM
35	Yes, the one leader took charge.	11/9/2017 11:43 PM
36	Parts, not all.	11/9/2017 11:25 PM

37	No	11/9/2017 11:18 PM
38	No, I moved on.	11/9/2017 11:01 PM
39	No	11/9/2017 10:51 PM
40	No, due to time constraints, the team just moved forward to complete the project.	11/9/2017 10:47 PM
41	Yes	11/9/2017 10:11 PM
42	Not really	11/9/2017 9:56 PM
43	No	11/9/2017 9:48 PM
44	Yes	11/9/2017 9:32 PM
45	No	11/9/2017 9:29 PM
46	No	11/9/2017 9:21 PM
47	Yes	11/9/2017 9:12 PM
48	Not really	11/9/2017 9:01 PM
49	A new leader was selected	11/9/2017 8:56 PM
50	No, Not in the allotted time	11/9/2017 8:55 PM
51	Not really. I left the team and reported it, but from what I know it was never addressed.	11/9/2017 8:53 PM
52	Yes, but not soon enough to minimize negative influence to team members	11/9/2017 8:41 PM
53	Yes, I left the team (school)	11/9/2017 7:52 PM
54	No	11/9/2017 7:13 PM
55	No	11/9/2017 7:12 PM
56	No	11/9/2017 6:05 PM

57	Moved on from the team.	11/9/2017 6:04 PM
58	No	11/9/2017 5:56 PM
59	No, others had to pick up the slack	11/9/2017 5:39 PM
60	No	11/9/2017 5:16 PM
61	No	11/9/2017 5:11 PM
62	No	11/9/2017 5:10 PM
63	Everything is resolved when you have a can do attitude	11/9/2017 5:07 PM
64	Yes, boss was fired & I left the team.	11/9/2017 5:02 PM
65	No	11/9/2017 5:00 PM
66	Yes, team members addressed the issue with the leader. Many found new positions	11/9/2017 4:59 PM
67	No	11/9/2017 4:46 PM
68	Yes	11/9/2017 4:44 PM
69	No	11/9/2017 4:40 PM
70	Does just choosing to do it myself and stop depending on "team them", count as resolved? If not, then no, never resolved.	11/9/2017 4:39 PM
71	Yes	11/9/2017 4:33 PM
72	Never	11/9/2017 4:32 PM
73	No	11/9/2017 4:27 PM
74	Yes, she quit! Which increased the team's moral and doing the former teammate's duties was less stressful.	11/9/2017 4:25 PM
75	Not yet	11/9/2017 4:18 PM
76	Yes with conditions attached.	11/9/2017 4:12 PM

77	Not yet, still in the midst of it.	11/9/2017 3:56 PM
78	The individuals dissolved themselves, or they were termi-nated due to their actions.	11/9/2017 3:53 PM
79	Yes	11/9/2017 3:38 PM
80	No	11/9/2017 3:18 PM
81	Normally not with a team. I end of covering or leading the pack.	11/9/2017 2:31 PM
82	No	11/9/2017 1:52 PM
83	N/A	11/9/2017 1:11 PM
84	Yes I left the Team	11/9/2017 1:01 PM
85	Yes, in the sense others picked up the slack and completed the task. The person's name was simply deleted from the group's name.	11/9/2017 12:03 PM
86	Yes	11/9/2017 12:03 PM
87	Problemas de equipo y de todo un poco	11/9/2017 11:26 AM
88	Yes, after open discussion.	11/9/2017 10:43 AM
89	Yes	11/9/2017 10:28 AM
90	Yes	11/9/2017 10:27 AM
91	Yes	11/9/2017 10:19 AM
92	Not really	11/9/2017 10:08 AM
93	No the team member remained on our team as we com-pleted our weekly team papers not fairly doing her part but doing more than done previously	11/9/2017 6:36 AM
94	Nope	11/9/2017 12:34 AM
95	Ironically, the person had to leave the team unexpectedly.	11/8/2017 11:50 PM

96	Yeah ... I sued for harassment	11/8/2017 8:51 PM
97	No	11/8/2017 7:46 PM
98	No	11/8/2017 7:45 PM
99	Unable to answer #2 since #1 wasn't worded appropriately.	11/8/2017 5:38 PM
100	Yes	11/8/2017 12:19 PM
101	No	11/8/2017 11:17 AM
102	Yes....next time I teamed up with a more proactive group.	11/8/2017 11:13 AM
103	Not really— separation of assignments	11/8/2017 10:48 AM
104	Its still an ongoing issue	11/8/2017 10:38 AM
105	Not really, the business was dissolved	11/8/2017 10:25 AM
106	No	11/8/2017 10:17 AM
107	No.	11/8/2017 10:16 AM
108	Yes	11/8/2017 9:54 AM
109	Yes	11/8/2017 9:51 AM
110	Yes, once others saw what I saw, the person was confronted and reported to lead.	11/8/2017 9:48 AM
111	Yes, they worked as hard as I did	11/8/2017 9:27 AM
112	No,	11/8/2017 8:39 AM
113	No	11/8/2017 8:14 AM
114	On the surface it was	11/8/2017 7:58 AM
115	Rarely	11/8/2017 7:27 AM

116	No	11/8/2017 6:29 AM
117	No	11/8/2017 5:16 AM
118	It's ongoing	11/8/2017 12:54 AM
119	In basketball know we never won more than two games each season. In the work or school setting the group eventually got things together but it was just a lot of time wasted.	11/8/2017 12:53 AM
120	Sometimes	11/8/2017 12:24 AM
121	No	11/8/2017 12:08 AM
122	No	11/7/2017 10:58 PM
123	Not really	11/7/2017 10:57 PM
124	Yes, she was replaced. My best	11/7/2017 10:52 PM
125	No	11/7/2017 10:43 PM

Q3 WHAT WAS YOUR BEST EXPERIENCE WITH A TEAM

Answered: 125   Skipped: 0

#	RESPONSES	DATE
1	Working with a group of high performers.	11/21/2017 2:19 PM
2	Everyone was knowledgeable in their area, timely and had no issue with another team member	11/16/2017 12:28 PM
3	My best experience with a team that I put together was the commitment of each person to accomplish the job with the spirit of excellence.	11/13/2017 6:42 AM
4	When everyone comes in ready to produce top quality work to see the project through, because they are all on board with the same intentions in sharing the vision of producing work well done. The shared passion made it happen.	11/13/2017 5:34 AM
5	Hopefully this one.	11/12/2017 2:24 PM
6	Completing the task in an efficient & timely manner	11/10/2017 1:55 PM
7	Everyone contributes utilizing individual talents.	11/10/2017 1:02 PM
8	Meeting/exceeding goals	11/10/2017 10:39 AM
9	Present team where everybody pulls their weight, conflicts are resolved, all are trusted to do their work not micro-managed, and we check in on each other as whole people	11/10/2017 8:51 AM
10	a successfully completed project with full participation and input from all	11/10/2017 8:31 AM
11	Working together in sync! Everyone completed their portion and we communicated very well.	11/10/2017 7:58 AM
12	Everyone worked collectively together without trying to outdo one another. Assisting each other when someone was stronger in something where another may have been weaker.	11/10/2017 7:45 AM
13	In my previous role as an Administrator, partnering with the Medical Director and Nurse Manager. We were aligned and communicated well.	11/10/2017 7:44 AM

14	All tasks were completed and we didn't have any disagreements that we're not resolved	11/10/2017 7:41 AM
15	When everyone was enthusiastic about the project and also willing to learn what strengths each member contributed	11/10/2017 7:39 AM
16	Unit cohesion	11/10/2017 7:37 AM
17	Working with a team of people who all enjoyed serving and helping each other out.	11/10/2017 7:06 AM
18	Current job, all five of us work together. Always help each other out. Truly believe that "we are all in this together"	11/10/2017 7:04 AM
19	Collaborate members with innovative award winning solutions	11/10/2017 6:26 AM
20	The final product	11/10/2017 6:24 AM
21	When we had a crisis and was short of staff, everyone assisted to resolve the problem.	11/10/2017 6:19 AM
22	Working with a group of contractor that could fill gaps for one another that truly worked as a team	11/10/2017 6:15 AM
23	I was partnering with a business on their expansion. I had to call on a number of HR partners to pull this though (recruitment, compensation, HR managers, business leads). We were trying to also ensure we were meeting our diversity goals with the our hiring and all by a very short timeline. We met the timelines and exceeded our diversity goals...a true partnership.	11/10/2017 6:15 AM
24	Being associated with individuals smarter/better than you send just as hungry and excited about what you're doing together	11/10/2017 6:14 AM
25	Everyone working together and following through	11/10/2017 6:01 AM
26	Winning	11/10/2017 5:59 AM
27	Everyone totally committed to winning a championship!	11/10/2017 5:54 AM
28	Pulling off a great PD for coworkers	11/10/2017 1:44 AM
29	Meeting our goals	11/10/2017 1:37 AM

30	Working together and completing a great presentation or project	11/10/2017 12:51 AM
31	A team of responsible individuals	11/10/2017 12:19 AM
32	Communication and follow through	11/10/2017 12:18 AM
33	When everyone pulled their weight & completed their specific task	11/10/2017 12:05 AM
34	A team with stellar communication and respect for the others on the time.	11/9/2017 11:46 PM
35	Everyone collaborated.	11/9/2017 11:43 PM
36	Working together towards a common goal. Having each other's backs by sharing knowledge, and discussing challenges which ultimately produced great discovery and process improvement.	11/9/2017 11:25 PM
37	Everyone showing up on time and doing their part	11/9/2017 11:18 PM
38	As a new administrator @ a new school, I was respected for my focused professional development training and feedback. I worked with people who wanted to improve.	11/9/2017 11:01 PM
39	people who are collaborative, could agree to disagree, and yet still achieved the task at hand	11/9/2017 10:51 PM
40	No egos involved. Everyone willing to do more than expected.	11/9/2017 10:47 PM
41	Everyone participating	11/9/2017 10:11 PM
42	Making our deadline	11/9/2017 9:56 PM
43	When I felt I made a noticeable positive impact on others	11/9/2017 9:48 PM
44	Collaboration, like minds, equal contribution.	11/9/2017 9:32 PM
45	Having support from others	11/9/2017 9:29 PM
46	Good synergy and meeting all objectives	11/9/2017 9:21 PM
47	When each member was asked to detail % of work performed by each team member.11/9/2017 9:12 PM	
48	Lifelong friends and support	11/9/2017 9:01 PM

49	When everyone work together	11/9/2017 8:56 PM
50	Achieving the goal	11/9/2017 8:55 PM
51	I've had a few. Two that come to mind were both teams that came together for a competition. Everyone was driven with the same work ethic and desire to win. And we did.	11/9/2017 8:53 PM
52	Leader who valued and recognized each team member. recognized exemplary and most improved performance	11/9/2017 8:41 PM
53	Everyone dividing up the work , conquering the mission , coming back together to check one another, and finally putting all the pieces together!	11/9/2017 7:52 PM
54	Accomplishing the goal we set out to do as a team	11/9/2017 7:13 PM
55	A servant leader who knew how to engage the team and make everyone feel important by trusting them to do their part.	11/9/2017 7:12 PM
56	We all clicked instantly and were able to delegate tasks	11/9/2017 6:05 PM
57	Best is EntreprenewHer	11/9/2017 6:04 PM
58	Combing resources and expertise to create informative presentations	11/9/2017 5:56 PM
59	Approaching a difficult task and collaborating to find the best solution	11/9/2017 5:39 PM
60	Planning a career day	11/9/2017 5:16 PM
61	Work related committee	11/9/2017 5:11 PM
62	Cohesion	11/9/2017 5:10 PM
63	Figuring things out when you sit on leadership teams	11/9/2017 5:07 PM
64	An inspirational leader & great espirit de corps.	11/9/2017 5:02 PM
65	Finishing task sooner than required	11/9/2017 5:00 PM
66	Team members supporting each other and collaborating and sharing best practices to elevate the team	11/9/2017 4:59 PM
67	When a task meets the strengths of group members	11/9/2017 4:46 PM

68	Getting a project completed	11/9/2017 4:44 PM
69	Work outing team sports event	11/9/2017 4:40 PM
70	The day one of the organizations I'm a member of came together on a community project and everyone worked together in the true sense of team, to complete the project we committed to do.	11/9/2017 4:39 PM
71	Great leader	11/9/2017 4:33 PM
72	Full participation	11/9/2017 4:32 PM
73	American Institutes of Research (AIR) national team of technical advisors. We hailed from every part of the US, but we got things done!	11/9/2017 4:27 PM
74	Working in a kitchen with other women and everyone pitches in and does what they do best. No chiefs, just Indians!	11/9/2017 4:25 PM
75	Having a leader who understood the balance of being available when needed and backing off when the team was performing well	11/9/2017 4:18 PM
76	Several- small groups; not over 10!	11/9/2017 4:12 PM
77	When multiple personalities and talents balance each other towards a common goal.11/9/2017 3:56 PM	
78	Being blessed with a group of individuals who were sensitive my needs, and to the time difference when I was called to California during my father's last days. I am ever grateful for those people.	11/9/2017 3:53 PM
79	Thinking out of the box	11/9/2017 3:38 PM
80	Everyone going above and beyond to achieve resolution	11/9/2017 3:18 PM
81	I was on a team once where I was NOT the leader and everyone did what was expected in excellence! This was less stressful and a delight in the end!	11/9/2017 2:31 PM
82	Working together to meet a common goal	11/9/2017 1:52 PM
83	We were able to establish a hierarchy that defined the team roles therefore everyone could work within their role.	11/9/2017 1:11 PM
84	Growth and income for all	11/9/2017 1:01 PM

85	Everyone participated, with enthusiasm and the task took less time than anticipated.	11/9/2017 12:03 PM
86	Winning	11/9/2017 12:03 PM
87	Que hemos logrado el objetivo planeado	11/9/2017 11:26 AM
88	Feeling the high of successfully achieving an outcome	11/9/2017 10:43 AM
89	Meeting all our objectives, with happy members who got it.	11/9/2017 10:28 AM
90	When everyone knew their responsibility and worked in their respective area.	11/9/2017 10:27 AM
91	Creativity	11/9/2017 10:19 AM
92	Being heard and changed were implemented	11/9/2017 10:08 AM
93	Same masters program team paper experience but team roles and responsibilities identified, ownership was taken by each, the online teaming environment was as if we at the table together working on the paper sharing freely without judging ensuring excellence in all aspects. Team consensus was the objective for changes in direction	11/9/2017 6:36 AM
94	Developing a program with everyone on task	11/9/2017 12:34 AM
95	Working as a family. Everyone fully participated	11/8/2017 11:50 PM
96	Really haven't had any outstanding experience	11/8/2017 8:51 PM
97	Confronting the person that wasn't willing to share.	11/8/2017 7:46 PM
98	Teammate who was a true partner and cheerleader	11/8/2017 7:45 PM
99	Best experience was being present for an unexpected win.	11/8/2017 5:38 PM
100	Being part of it and having others to talk to who share your same experiences and can share how they handled the challenges	11/8/2017 12:19 PM
101	Working as one	11/8/2017 11:17 AM
102	Setting financial goals together to expa d a project and we exceeded that goal.	11/8/2017 11:13 AM

103	How ideas flourished and were executed	11/8/2017 10:48 AM
104	Working with my travel team. They are very supportive and willing to work together to achieve your goals.	11/8/2017 10:38 AM
105	The ideas that were created	11/8/2017 10:25 AM
106	Diversity. Great ideas, everyone worked together to achieve an excellent product.	11/8/2017 10:17 AM
107	Connecting with like-minded people.	11/8/2017 10:16 AM
108	Everyone pitched in did what we had to do to get the project done	11/8/2017 9:54 AM
109	Where everyone did their part and were truly engaged.	11/8/2017 9:51 AM
110	A joint effort of pulling off a citywide community event with much praise from others.	11/8/2017 9:48 AM
111	National integration of an IT system	11/8/2017 9:27 AM
112	Strong results when everyone contribute to the outcome	11/8/2017 8:39 AM
113	Collaboration, different experiences	11/8/2017 8:14 AM
114	When everyone truly wanted what was best for the group and not just themselves	11/8/2017 7:58 AM
115	So rare i can't remember	11/8/2017 7:27 AM
116	Teams where everyone understands and works toward a common goal.	11/8/2017 6:29 AM
117	In children sports when parents organize and coordinate	11/8/2017 5:16 AM
118	Cooperation, collegiality, &effective communication	11/8/2017 12:54 AM
119	In the work environment when I ran the team and I had much more control, was able to delegate tasks based on strengths and job description.	11/8/2017 12:53 AM
120	When expectations are met	11/8/2017 12:24 AM
121	Working with a well matched group with different strengths. We each used our gifts to produce an amazing event!	11/8/2017 12:08 AM

122	Complete synergy, produced 3 separate businesses.	11/7/2017 10:58 PM
123	Project completed on time within budget	11/7/2017 10:57 PM
124	My best experience with a team was a master level class project with teams of four. Experience was great since everyone did exactly what they were assigned and stayed in their lane. We put our parts together to make an awesome project.	11/7/2017 10:52 PM
125	When we all worked together. PSI-7	11/7/2017 10:43 PM

Q4 HOW DID EITHER EVENT SHAPE YOUR THOUGHTS AROUND TEAMS?

Answered: 125   Skipped: 0

#	RESPONSES	DATE
1	Knowing that when I became a leader I would need to deal with poor and high performers.	11/21/2017 2:19 PM
2	You have to demonstrate emotional intelligence when dealing with team members and the leadership to quickly address disruptive behavior.	11/16/2017 12:28 PM
3	See #1	11/13/2017 6:42 AM
4	Overall it has granted me the insight to decide if I can work on a particular team or not. It has helped me to pick up on potential kinks early in the project, and to correct those kinks before they derail the project. It has helped me to identify when role positions need changing in order to match the best people with the proper tasks of their strong points. This certainly helps the project to have positive results.	11/13/2017 5:34 AM
5	It made me not want to join any other group, until now, I've come across	11/12/2017 2:24 PM
6	Know who you are working with so things can be distributed equally	11/10/2017 1:55 PM
7	I prefer to work alone.	11/10/2017 1:02 PM
8	I still believe in teamwork	11/10/2017 10:39 AM
9	I've learned from both: what works and what doesn't. I've learned how much I can tolerate. I am learning to trust God in all circumstances, and that He will deliver me.	11/10/2017 8:51 AM
10	When it works it's great, but not everyone wants to be a team player	11/10/2017 8:31 AM
11	I still think it's stressful because if someone is not pulling his/ her weight it falls on the rest of the group.	11/10/2017 7:58 AM
12	The first event stated made me dislike group projects. The second stated, made me optimistic that all group projects are not like the first.	11/10/2017 7:45 AM
13	Communication is key to success.	11/10/2017 7:44 AM

14	It caused me to reconsider who is on my team and to plan better for slackers.	11/10/2017 7:41 AM
15	That there will always be those that work harder and sometimes, not so much.	11/10/2017 7:39 AM
16	Your input matters	11/10/2017 7:37 AM
17	It helped me understand the importance of being open to other's ideas and being willing to compromise my own in order for the sake of the team working cohesively.	11/10/2017 7:06 AM
18	No real impact. I try not to let the past influence my present. Once it's over I move on.	11/10/2017 7:04 AM
19	A team is only as effective as its members	11/10/2017 6:26 AM
20	To be a good team player you must be a good follower	11/10/2017 6:24 AM
21	Overall, I've been blessed to work with great teams. If I had all good teams, I wouldn't know how to work through the challenging ones.	11/10/2017 6:19 AM
22	I'll do teams, but only with people I KNOW 1) know their stuff 2) have the interest and ability to complete the assignment or 3) are willing workers, but don't want to/can't lead in which case I'll take the lead	11/10/2017 6:15 AM
23	I've always been a big collaborator, so my thoughts about team has not changed. I believe you always achieve better results when you are inclusive and collaborative. There is no "I" in "TEAM."	11/10/2017 6:15 AM
24	To be more cognizant of who you team up with.	11/10/2017 6:14 AM
25	Teamwork makes the dream work	11/10/2017 6:01 AM
26	Yes	11/10/2017 5:59 AM
27	Team are important to teach cooperation and teamwork.	11/10/2017 5:54 AM
28	There's a lot of compromise needed in teams. I like to sit back and see the direction of the team, and assess how effective it appears to be. If effective I'm okay not taking the lead. However, if it seems that the group is moving without direction, I tend to take the lead or begin creating a plan of action that most can "buy" into.	11/10/2017 1:44 AM
29	I still like being a part of one	11/10/2017 1:37 AM

30	I don't like to but I will	11/10/2017 12:51 AM
31	Look for the strengths of individuals, when making assignments.	11/10/2017 12:19 AM
32	Rather work alone and mentors to assist or give input	11/10/2017 12:18 AM
33	You need to know how to designated which task to who. Find out what their expertise is that will coincide with the skill set for the team in order for the end result to be A-plus	11/10/2017 12:05 AM
34	I believe teams can work using effective open communication	11/9/2017 11:46 PM
35	People want to be known for being involved but doesn't necessarily want to do the work.	11/9/2017 11:43 PM
36	There are good teams comprised of good people. The tools you employ can make or break your outcome and shape your overall experience.	11/9/2017 11:25 PM
37	I like working alone	11/9/2017 11:18 PM
38	Began studying how to manage staff through change.	11/9/2017 11:01 PM
39	That you have to be flexible, patient, and pull your weight, and make sure that you are adding value	11/9/2017 10:51 PM
40	Teams are simply a fact of life. And since you are dealing with individuals, there is absolutely every combination of experiences that one can have. So, the goal is simply to get to the end of the task, by any means necessary.	11/9/2017 10:47 PM
41	It can be done	11/9/2017 10:11 PM
42	I still don't like them	11/9/2017 9:56 PM
43	I make sure everyone feels heard	11/9/2017 9:48 PM
44	Requires you to think outside the box, utilize individual skills based on strengths and reassign responsibility based on weaknesses. Dimensional management.	11/9/2017 9:32 PM
45	I don't mind being in a team as long as most people are willing to do their part	11/9/2017 9:29 PM
46	Teams are doable but I'm an introvert	11/9/2017 9:21 PM
47	I abhor Group Projects.	11/9/2017 9:12 PM

48	I appreciate the team anyway. Parts will always work.	11/9/2017 9:01 PM
49	Supportive	11/9/2017 8:56 PM
50	Accentuated the need to choose team members wisely	11/9/2017 8:55 PM
51	The negative one is more recent but also I've had several similar experiences. It's made me much more cautious about the groups I work with. They must be "equally yoked" in knowledge and integrity.	11/9/2017 8:53 PM
52	The ineffective leader made it difficult for me to manage my team. they all wanted to be a slacker like the big cheese.	11/9/2017 8:41 PM
53	People need to be taught (sometimes) how to work together.	11/9/2017 7:52 PM
54	it didn't	11/9/2017 7:13 PM
55	I prefer to lead now and am cautious when asked to join a team	11/9/2017 7:12 PM
56	I do not like group work.	11/9/2017 6:05 PM
57	EntrepreNewHer helped shape my business	11/9/2017 6:04 PM
58	I prefer to work alone. But I can work in a team environment	11/9/2017 5:56 PM
59	I love teams, but clear objectives and expectations should be established initially.	11/9/2017 5:39 PM
60	I don't like being responsible/accountable for the work/behavior of others	11/9/2017 5:16 PM
61	They both reminded me that compromise in a group is essential in most cases.	11/9/2017 5:11 PM
62	I'd rather work by myself	11/9/2017 5:10 PM
63	It causes you to be more flexible and understanding when it comes to working it multiple people	11/9/2017 5:07 PM
64	Very clear lines between a boss & inspirational leader.	11/9/2017 5:02 PM
65	I realized everyone doesn't give 100% in every aspect	11/9/2017 5:00 PM
66	I enjoy working in teams however I ensure expectations are clear and the intent is known	11/9/2017 4:59 PM

67	Some teams work and others don't such is life	11/9/2017 4:46 PM
68	The success of a team depends on the mindset of the parties involved. Being open to others ideas and opinions can go a long way when attempting to accomplish a goal.	11/9/2017 4:44 PM
69	I generally love team work	11/9/2017 4:40 PM
70	I still think the best team where my businesses/interests directly are concerned is the team of "me, myself and I", as it seems only when people get constant praise or tons of funds with very little work that others are true team members.	11/9/2017 4:39 PM
71	Greater awareness on my role in a team	11/9/2017 4:33 PM
72	Prefer to work alone and be responsible for the outcome of a project	11/9/2017 4:32 PM
73	While initially having a disdain for teams, I did experience a really positive outcome with a particular team	11/9/2017 4:27 PM
74	It helps to know your teammate's strengths and weaknesses upfront so assignment of duties is easier and expectations can be better managed.	11/9/2017 4:25 PM
75	The bad experiences have taught me some coping mechanisms when dealing with weak leadership	11/9/2017 4:18 PM
76	No impact!	11/9/2017 4:12 PM
77	Sometimes it works out and sometimes it doesn't. That's life.	11/9/2017 3:56 PM
78	Both experiences affirmed what I have believed about the collective-Whether it's voting, or a community service project, if people are not equal stakeholders in a common effort, it will falter.	11/9/2017 3:53 PM
79	Their is NO I in team	11/9/2017 3:38 PM
80	Usually prefer to work independently	11/9/2017 3:18 PM
81	I do not like teams as you never know what you are going to get	11/9/2017 2:31 PM
82	I know to focus on my job within the team and focus on the task	11/9/2017 1:52 PM
83	Working on a team is not my preferred method but you can't do everything alone.	11/9/2017 1:11 PM

84	Be all in	11/9/2017 1:01 PM
85	The negative has given me the sense to always be prepared to pick up someone else's slack and remain positive.	11/9/2017 12:03 PM
86	I don't like teams	11/9/2017 12:03 PM
87	Organizando y delagando	11/9/2017 11:26 AM
88	I've been scarred by the bad experiences, but the positives have given me renewed hope in working hard, positive mindsets and the satisfaction of achievement.	11/9/2017 10:43 AM
89	Similarity in interest, passions and outcomes are critical to success	11/9/2017 10:28 AM
90	That I work well with teams and that all being a part of the collaborative process worked best.	11/9/2017 10:27 AM
91	I needed to be open to listening everyone's ideas, even though I do not always agree	11/9/2017 10:19 AM
92	To make sure I speak up and be heard	11/9/2017 10:08 AM
93	Who is on the team matters, rules of engagement need to be set upfront, the end objective must stay top of mind, and regardless of any slack in team members someone has to be willing to take up the slack to keep it moving without adding bitterness in the mix	11/9/2017 6:36 AM
94	I'm more conscious of what people do, not what they say	11/9/2017 12:34 AM
95	The negative experience turned me against working in a team, but the positive experience renewed my trust in collaboration.	11/8/2017 11:50 PM
96	Negative	11/8/2017 8:51 PM
97	Dead weight needs to be eliminated.	11/8/2017 7:46 PM
98	Important to be a partner and teammate. Volunteer to help without being asked	11/8/2017 7:45 PM
99	My thoughts were impacted positively - eagerly wanted to attend more games	11/8/2017 5:38 PM
100	Positive that it's better to work as a team than an island	11/8/2017 12:19 PM
101	Working together helps	11/8/2017 11:17 AM

102	It made me more selective of whom I team up with in projects. I base my team selection on results of my teammates.	11/8/2017 11:13 AM
103	Realized everyone was an individual and respected their execution to a project that benefited the entire business.	11/8/2017 10:48 AM
104	I know going into a team environment to be sure to keep my expectations low and be willing to step in and do the work.	11/8/2017 10:38 AM
105	It made me want to really think about what characteristics to look for when wanting to choose a team/partner on a project	11/8/2017 10:25 AM
106	Depending on who's on the team will determined how i work and what i expect.	11/8/2017 10:17 AM
107	Both experiences displayed the difference between customized and generic teams. The former is far more effective.	11/8/2017 10:16 AM
108	Set expectations on how everyone is to contribute	11/8/2017 9:54 AM
109	I don't necessarily like being on teams of more than 3-4 people.	11/8/2017 9:51 AM
110	We bonded and had a renewed others faith in each other. Lead to more communication and trust within the team.	11/8/2017 9:48 AM
111	Bring people together through engagement	11/8/2017 9:27 AM
112	Luv to work on teams. Just have to communicate the vision and hold people accountable to their contributions	11/8/2017 8:39 AM
113	Still don't like teams. Like my own pace	11/8/2017 8:14 AM
114	It makes me cautious about the "personalities" in that group	11/8/2017 7:58 AM
115	not a fan...the smaller the group the better the team	11/8/2017 7:27 AM
116	Teamwork is the only way to grow.	11/8/2017 6:29 AM
117	Prefer individual sports	11/8/2017 5:16 AM
118	I know what it feels like to be on effective team & what it feels like not to be	11/8/2017 12:54 AM

119	I generally like working in teams. Usually I am the head of the team by default. Overall it helps lighten the load and get things done. You also learn from each member, and has a team leader you can help bring each team members strengths.	11/8/2017 12:53 AM
120	I am less trusting of team, greater micro management	11/8/2017 12:24 AM
121	Unfortunately my bad experiences far outweigh my good ones. I dread teams and prefer solo contributions.	11/8/2017 12:08 AM
122	Neither did	11/7/2017 10:58 PM
123	More upfront roles identified, collaboration, and what's in it for team	11/7/2017 10:57 PM
124	First event didn't deter me from teams, just made reminded me to ensure that all team members clear of their role, and if not willing to carry that role out, remove as soon as possible.	11/7/2017 10:52 PM
125	It made me see what has possible when we all worked together	11/7/2017 10:43 PM

RESULTS DRIVEN TEAMS CHECKLIST

The concept of team is vital to success in any organization, and team building is part of every manager's role.

RESULTS DRIVEN TEAMS

- Increased efficiency

- Idea Generation

- Learning Experience

- Enhanced Communication

- Share the workload

- Support network

- Makes Work Fun

- Creates Healthy Competition

CHARACTERISTICS OF A RESULTS DRIVEN TEAM

- They have Emotional Intelligence

- They have a good mix of introverts and extroverts

- They share and understand their common goals

- They make time for humor

- They communicate proactively

- They have strong leadership at the helm

- Ability To Stand The Test Of Time

QUALITIES OF A RESULTS DRIVEN TEAM MEMBER

- They show genuine commitment

- They are flexible

- They move out of the shadows

- They are reliable and responsible

- They listen actively

- They keep their team informed

- They are always ready to help

- They support and respect others

- They are problem solvers

- They recognize when they are wrong

- They don't brag

- They don't blame others

QUALITIES OF A RESULTS DRIVEN TEAM LEADER

- Visioning: Effective team leaders need to establish a clear vision for the future

- Delegating: Team leaders must be good at delegating

- Engaging: Successful team leaders must be able to embrace their members as people, as well as workers

- Communicating: Successful team leaders are also excellent communicators

- Problem-solving: The best leaders are also effective problems solvers

- Decision-making: Effective leaders also are able to make timely decisions

- Coaching and mentoring: All successful team leaders are also good coaches

- Acting with integrity: Successful leaders can be counted on, to tell the truth, and be a living example of their team's core values

- Negotiating: Team leaders utilize negotiation skills to achieve results and reach an understanding

- Ability to influence: A leader needs to be able to rally the team when need be

- Ability to adapt to change: The only certainty in life is uncertainty; learning how to cope with it will be necessary

About Dr. Taunya Lowe

Dr. Taunya Lowe, known as *'The Riot Starter'* is an innovative, insightful, change agent who understands the concept of adding value to others. As a trainer and presenter, she is witty and engaging while offering practical solutions, healing the pain points around team progression and productivity, succession planning, and professional development. She uses a cadre of assessments to establish baselines within organizations, such as the Maxwell Leadership Game, Wiley DiSC, and 360 assessments. She offers training coaching and consulting using her results-driven philosophy back by 20 years of research to help organizations create High-Performance Workplaces. A national and international speaker, trainer, author, podcaster, mindset coach, and consultant. Dr. Taunya Lowe is a graduate of Clark Atlanta University and Capella University. She is the founder and driving force behind the Results-Driven Philosophy and the Riot Starter movement, which consists of programs, products, retreats, and trainings. She is inspirational, transformational, and your partner for individual and organizational success. http://www.drtaunyalowe.com

Gratitude

"You can do what I cannot do, I can do what you cannot do. Together we can do great things."

-- Mother Teresa

I am very grateful to collaborate with the family of Randy Glasbergen and the Glasbergen Cartoon Service for the use of the cartoons at the end of each chapter. There's nothing like a little humor to get the point across.

Participants in the 2017 Pros and Cons of Teams Survey, I thank you for your honesty about teams, and providing what it takes for teams to thrive well in an organization.

Thank you to my coaches: Reggie Hammond, Lisa Nichols, Susie Carder, and James Malinchak. Your presence, mentoring and guidance in my life, helps me to make a difference in the lives of others.

Thank you to my Mastermind group members, accountability partners, and colleagues for your motivation, support and encouragement.

Thank you to "The Riot Starters", my clients, thank you for the opportunity to hold your feet to the fire and hold you accountable to meet your individual and organizational goals and to "stay started", it was a reminder for me to "stay started" as well.

I am eternally grateful for my team: Phoebe with WeEmpower Virtual Professionals, Log0folio and Joy Glorioso for the book cover design, Rosa at Dream Books Formatting and the countless number of people who read the galley copy and provided feedback, suggestions. Each person brought an amazing gift and skill to the process to help me produce a quality product: Deborah Miller, Dr. Jamille Richardson, Dr. Gale Belton Topping, Tana M. Sessions and Eric G. Reid..

Thank you to my family, friends who are like family, and those who love me unconditionally. Thank you for understanding the late nights, the long days and the missed events because I was creating in the lab. Thank you for making sure that I ate, stayed hydrated, stretched, worked out and laughing with hilarious memes.

If you are reading this page at this very moment I want you to know that I am grateful to you because you are committed to what it takes to create a high performing workplace.

Ask About Our Programs & Services

RESULTS DRIVEN PHILOSOPHY TRAINING

- Mindset
- Strategy
- Leadership
- Team Building
- Customer Experience
- Sales

RESULTS DRIVEN PHILOSOPHY COACHING

RESULTS DRIVEN PHILOSOPHY CONSULTING

RESULTS DRIVEN PHILOSOPHY ASSESSMENT PACKAGES

TO CONTACT DR. TAUNYA LOWE:

678-451-4259
support@drtaunyalowe.com
www.drtaunyalowe.com

SPECIAL FREE BONUS GIFT FOR YOU!

I'd like to offer you a special FREE

4-part series bonus gift on

The 4 Keys to a High Performance Workplace

www.FreeGiftFromTaunya.com

Get Your Free Extra BONUS Gift ($997 Value)
www.FreeGiftFromTaunya.com

If you're ready to positively transform your life, then read and absorb the strategies in this brilliant book by my friend Dr. Taunya Lowe! Dr. Lowe truly cares about helping others and her ideas will make a positive difference in your life!"

- James Malinchak, Featured on ABCs Hit TV Show, "Secret Millionaire"
Authored 20 Books, Delivered 3,000 Presentations & 1,000 Consultations
Best-Selling Author, Millionaire Success Secrets
Founder, www.MillionaireFreeBook.com

Dr. Taunya Lowe is masterful at helping employees self-identify their workplace behavior challenges and build a strategy for improved performance and success.

- Joe Theismann
Legendary NFL World Champion Quarterback & NFL Football TV Commentator

As a partner to your success, Dr. Taunya Lowe adds value to your organization using her expertise while integrating real life experiences into her methodology.

- Kevin Harrington, Original Shark on the Hit TV Show Shark Tank,
Pioneer of the As Seen on TV Industry

Dr. Taunya Lowe's Results Driven Philosophy will transform your organization one department at a time.

- Patty Aubery, #1 NY Times Best Selling Author
Past President, Chicken Soup for the Soul
Co-Founder, The Jack Canfield Companies

This book is the secret weapon that every organization and leader can use to achieve success in business. Dr. Lowe has put together a collection of the four keys and organizational success strategies, in an easy to read guide. Her book is incredibly noteworthy and valuable to help you achieve a high-performance workplace and the results that every business and organization strives for to be successful. "Results Driven Organizations" is truly magical! Well done!

- John Formica (The Ex-Disney Guy)
One of the World's Foremost Disney Philosophy Experts
America's Best Customer Experience Speaker, Trainer, Coach

ISBN 978-164316921-7

This fast-moving book is based on practical, proven strategies you can use immediatley to get better results in your business.

- Brian Tracy
Author/Speaker & President, Brian Tracey International